PAUL VIOLI

REBEL ARTS

Published in the United States of America in September 2014
by Rebel Arts, an imprint of Gingko Press, Inc.

Gingko Press, Inc.
1321 Fifth Street
Berkeley, CA 94710
www.gingkopress.com

Paperback: 978-1-934471-02-9
Hardcover: 978-1-934471-01-2

First printing

In Baltic Circles was originally published by the Kulchur Foundation.
Harmatan and *Splurge* were originally published by SUN.
Likewise, *The Curious Builder*, *Fracas*, and *Overnight* were originally
published by Hanging Loose Press.

Book design and cover design: Anna Dütschler

Printed in Germany

Library of Congress Cataloging-in-Publication Data

Violi, Paul, 1944-2011.
[Poems. Selections]
Selected poems, 1970-2007 / Paul Violi ; edited by Charles North and Tony Towle.
    pages ; cm
Includes index.
ISBN 978-1-934471-01-2 (hardcover) -- ISBN 978-1-934471-02-9 (pbk.)
I. North, Charles, 1941- II. Towle, Tony, 1939- III. Title.
PS3572.I59A6 2014
811'.54--dc23
                    2014029803

Books by Paul Violi

POETRY

She'll Be Riding Six White Horses, 1970

Automatic Transmissions, 1970

Waterworks, 1972

In Baltic Circles, 1973
(reprinted 2011)

Some Poems, 1976

Harmatan, 1977

Splurge, 1982

Likewise, 1988

The Curious Builder, 1993

The Anamorphosis, 1995

Fracas, 1999

Breakers, 2000

Envoy: Life Is Completely Interesting, 2005

Overnight, 2007

The Tame Magpie, 2014

PROSE

Selected Accidents, Pointless Anecdotes, 2002

PAUL VIOLI

SELECTED POEMS

1970-2007

Edited by Charles North and Tony Towle

REBEL ARTS

Table of Contents

from **Likewise (1988)**

from **The Curious Builder (1993)**

from **Fracas (1998)**

from **Overnight (2007)**

Preface

Tony Towle

1.

I first became acquainted with Paul Violi when he began attending the poetry workshop I was conducting for the Poetry Project at St. Mark's Church in 1969-1970. By the spring semester, I had noticed that Paul was among the half-dozen students whose work stood out from the rest. There were other poets teaching workshops at St. Mark's at this time, and Paul attended many of them.

One of the people in my class with whom Paul became friendly was Charles North, whose poems, as it happened, I felt were also exceptional. In fact, by the end of the course, it seemed to me that both Charles and Paul were well on their way out of the "workshop attendee" category to becoming accomplished poets. The three of us kept in touch by mail after the workshop ended, and fairly soon the three-way relationship included personal socializing— we began meeting for drinks or coffee, where we "talked shop" and gossiped, and we got together with our respective families, as well. My "teacher" status soon dissolved into one-third of a peership that lasted until Paul's death, in 2011.

It was thus natural that Charles and I would have the responsibility— and the privilege—of choosing the poems for Paul's *Selected*, and it is a task that we have shared equally.

2.

I came to NY in 68. What excited me then—more in what painters like Rivers, Oldenburg, Dine, and later Grooms, were up to than poets—I still feel is valuable now, namely what made their paintings beautiful in spite of breaking all the rules. . . . What was crucial to me before that, while in my early twenties, was coming upon novelists like Amis, Donleavy, and Heller, along with reading the great satirists—Pope, Swift, Dryden, Voltaire, Rabelais, Byron.[1]

Paul grew up on Long Island and then attended Boston University, graduating in 1966 with a B.A. in English. Between college and coming to New York, where he established himself as a poet, came an overseas interlude that added an important component to his life experience, and to his future work. That December, Paul joined the Peace Corps and, after a training period in Mexico, was sent to the far northwestern part of Nigeria as a surveyor and mapmaker. His adventures over the next six months eventually coalesced into the poems of the book-length *Harmatan*. He left Nigeria soon after the onset of the Biafran revolt in June, 1967.

Then came an impromptu journey—odyssey, really—from West Africa to the Canary Islands, Spain, Italy and Greece, and a contiguous but unplanned route from Bulgaria through Turkey, Iran, Pakistan, Afghanistan and India, to Nepal—back to Europe, and finally to New York in April, 1968. Not only was Paul traveling on a (frayed) shoestring, but the trip was physically arduous and occasionally even life-threatening—as when he was sleeping on a train in India and thieves cut his dungarees open to steal his wallet.[2] In addition to *Harmatan*, poems and prose related to this sojourn made their way into his books over the next thirty-plus years.

3.

Paul's surviving "early work" consists of poems he wrote after his return to the United States that he self-published in two mimeo-graphed booklets in 1970. Often hastily composed and "young," the poems nonetheless show originality and wit. Several were reworked and appeared in his first substantial collection, *In Baltic Circles* (1973). The difference in the level of accomplishment bet-ween the contents of this volume and that of the mimeographed booklets is astonishing. By the time of *Splurge* (1982), Paul poem's were as impressive as those of anyone around.

The fundamentals of Paul's sensibility and concerns were there from the beginning: *I'm still bringing things into play that I started using back then* [in the 60s]—*mainly humor, being true to the way I see things, along with historical references, allusions, impersonating and adapting prose forms, retrieving narrative, fictional or imagined experiences, and being free to mix up the immiscible, the whole bag of serio-comic takes and tones.*

4.

"Impersonating and adapting prose forms" was one of Paul's most salient gifts. A few examples: "Triptych" (a parody of TV listings), "Exacta" (the calling of a horse race, the names of the horses being the supporting device), and "Index" (the absurd and hilarious reduction of an artist's life to synopsized entries at the back of an imaginary book)—from *Splurge*; and, from *The Curious Builder*, "Police Blotter," in which the officers (Paul's friends) respond to un-likely emergencies, and "Errata," in which improbable corrections are made to a nonexistent text. *When I do use such forms I assume I'm employing a simple metaphor, a familiar if not trite context yet a very accessible one, by which I don't mean to celebrate the ordinary but to subvert it.*

Subversion in a historical context is the basis for "House of Xerxes," in which the famous description by Herodotus of the Persian monarch's legendary million-man army crossing the Hellespont is described in the fatuous diction of a fashion runway show! (*Overnight*) "King Nasty" (*Likewise*) is a remarkable satire that features a crass movie producer giving an underling extemporaneous and detailed descriptions of proposed scenes in a film about an executioner during the French Revolution's Reign of Terror, which are both ghastly, and, in the Violi manner, funny in spite of the subject.

Paul could find inspiration in writers of the past, as well as events. In "Little Testament" (*Likewise*), he takes the concept of François Villon's famous poem of the same name and, using the latter's trademark *Item*, makes highly "creative" bequests. "More on the Heroic Deeds and Manner of the Worthy Rabelais, Doctor of Medicine" (*The Curious Builder*), is like a literary roast—a convincing parody of the language of *Gargantua* used in a send-up of its author.

There are other splendid longer poems in this volume, in addition to the several mentioned above: "One for the Monk of Montaudon" (*Splurge*), "Wet Bread and Roasted Pearls" (*The Curious Builder*), "The Hazards of Imagery" (*Fracas*), and "I.D." (*Overnight*), as well as a great many shorter gems that I don't have the space to name, but which the reader will certainly discover and appreciate.

5.

Paul lived in New York City from 1968 until 1970, and then moved with his wife, Ann, whom he had married in 1969, to the northern suburbs—first to Beacon, in Dutchess County; after two years, to Briarcliff, in Westchester; and finally, in 1977, to Putnam Valley, in Putnam County, where he spent the last thirty-four years of his life.

Paul had a plethora of jobs early on, but in the mid-'70s found his vocation: teaching. A part-time position at Bloomfield College, in New Jersey, led, over the years, to courses at a number of institutions, including New York and Columbia Universities, and New School University. (A complete list can be found in the Brief Chronology at the back of this book.)

The constant traveling by car to fulfill teaching assignments, necessitating trips between New Jersey, New York City, and Westchester, for example,—sometimes on the same or subsequent days—led to an "automotive" category in the Violi oeuvre, prime examples of which are "Extenuating Circumstances" and "On an Acura Integra" (*Fracas*); as well as a sub-genre: poems whose mise-en-scène (at least in the opening lines) is set in a diner or coffee shop (such as in "One for the Monk of Montaudon"), where he often found himself "killing time." The inconvenience and tedium caused by his work schedule led to some brilliant poems.

6.

Paul's style was never radical: *What mattered was not a clean wholesale break with the past but a continuing homage to or conversation with poetry I loved.* He did not work to exemplify theoretical concepts, on the one hand, or hold himself to an artificial standard of what poetry was *allowed* to be, on the other. In this respect, that of literary freedom, he can be very much identified with the New York School. Regardless of categorization, when I read Paul's work I feel excitement and pleasure, and a transport from the quotidian that is, to me, the ultimate worth of poetry.

---

[1] From an Interview of Paul Violi by Leo Edelstein for *Pataphysics* magazine, 2004, and reprinted on www.paulvioli.com. All Violi quotes—which appear italicized—are from this interview.

[2] Paul Violi, *Selected Accidents, Pointless Anecdotes*, Hanging Loose Press, 2002.

SELECTED POEMS

1970-2007

In Baltic Circles

PUBLIC WORKS

Swinburne pulls up to the light
with 35 screeching yellow cabs.
They rev their engines
the light turns red
they sound their horns
and off they go.

"Tally ho," yells Swinburne, "tally ho!"

Monet crosses the George Washington Bridge
without thinking about
our first President's dentures.
He could care less.
He drives slowly up the Palisades.
A flock of cabs passed him a long time ago.
It's 11:63 a.m. and he could care less.
It's a warm spring day
and the bugs splatter like snowflakes
against his windshield.
Soon it is covered with the multi-colored splotches.
He stops for gas.
When the attendant begins to clean the windshield
Monet can do one of two things: he either

(Hi, I'm Paul Violi and I'd like a word with you
about BIC pens. I've written some swell poems
with BIC pens and so has my wife, Ann. I expect
our child will really like BIC pens too. You know
how ordinary pens sometimes botch things up and
give you a glimpse of things to come like, well,
when I'm old and getting a bit, uh, senile, I suppose
my mind, like yours, neighbor, will skip a word

here and there, scratch a mere impression of what
should have been a fine thought on the page and,
in a manner of speaking, just plain run out of ink.
But there is no reason your pen has to falter like
that and you can bet BIC pens never will. So take
my advice, do yourself a favor and buy a BIC pen
today. Pick up a couple for the whole family while
you're at it and tell them I sent you!)

It's still a warm spring day
and a man waving
a square orange flag
diverts Monet into the outer lane.

Other men in red vests
have placed orange stanchions in the road,
another drives a blue truck at 3 miles per hour.
They follow him on foot, spraying white lines
and double white lines, yellow lines
and broken yellow lines while 3 men in black boots
chop up shiny casks of tar, melt it
and scribble the stuff over the cracks
in the pavement.
The gray concrete sparkles and its reflection hovers
over it like a mirage on the wrong road to wonderland.

The first to eat lunch
wipes his hands on a green T-shirt.
He steps off the road and examines a tomato
and cheese sandwich: "...I remember a job
we did near the shore, a parking lot.
My brother Harry worked that one.

So did my cousin and my nephew.
We laid down about an acre of asphalt
near the beach and I used to take my daughter
there at odd hours for driving lessons.

I explained to her how we had put down
a long white line and then angling into that one
a lot of short, slanted ones.
But she said it looked like the skeleton of a fish.
I couldn't teach her anything.
She lives in the city now. I think she's married.

But in the summer, it's packed on Sundays
and let me tell you something: when I see all the spaces
filled and the cars glittering like a fish on its side
in the sunlight, I want to tell you
it's no accident. I'm glad my brother convinced me
to take this job. It ain't all politics."

The rest of the men unpack their lunches.
Some exchange sandwiches, some of them drink orange
soda, others guzzle grape juice or beer.

The second crew has finished shoveling asphalt
off the back of the truck.
The paint is still drying,
all the holes in the road are now bumps.

SONNET FOR THE EARL OF SURREY

The golfer smiles in his polo shirt, the little
man has beaten the bully, the housewife is
using a new detergent and the Californian squints
behind his sunglasses; the man in the diner likes
his new bow tie and so does the doctor who saved
the injured cheerleader; the detective uses hair
tonic, the stout nurse is immaculate, the waitress
wants to date the truckdriver; the grocer slices
a pound of baloney, the reporter asks him how it
feels; the teacher wears a wild shirt, the coach
tells the youngster to shape up or ship out, the old
lady asks him the time, the woman in curlers orders
a hamburger and yet I want to jump for joy.

SUMMER

Spent some of the day
   holding a toad
spheres for eyes, black and gold.

Then put up the sheetrock and spackled
it with Myron, who showed up
   drunk every morning,
fired five times that week
   except Saturday,
everyone's drunk on Saturday.

Seth, a friend of his, took the precaution
of nailing his shoes to the scaffold
so when he fell he never hit the ground.

   . . . looked up later
to see him saw himself right off the roof.

Sixty years old. Carpenter.
Three dollars per hour. One black tooth in his mouth.

Old handmade nails and spikes,
   the planks pried up
      mephitic air.

   Surface of the floorboards rock hard
but the bottom rotten
grown back into the ground.
More planks pried up, innumerable insects
       frantic in the light.

And grimy, swearing workers
   walking away,
      hatched from the torn-down shed.

SLEEPING DACTYLS AND LURKING IAMBS

When I think how our love has been
slow and often tumultuous
like the process facing those who
want to radicalize public
housing management, I never
doubt its ultimate success will
have a very heavy impact.
Most especially if we work at it.

Just as these new urban poor will
be incorporated in the mainstream
of life, we will witness slight but
meaningful and lasting changes
which will reach a high level of involvement
as the exciting developments unfold.

TYRANNOSAURUS BRONX

for Allen Appel

All the elevated lakes are frozen
into the flat tar roofs of factories and schools
Air vents and chimney stacks
have been appointed plants by a metallic sun
The custodians swing their broad mops
down the vacant halls of the day's interior

The past recedes at the same rate
as the future and again leaves me high and dry
on a winter plateau that was formerly the Bronx

I relax with my head propped in my arms
watching the drowned choir that was once my toes
Their erased faces stand in unison
at the end of the bed as the Bronx begins
to revolve around a stationary record
like smoke over a doused fire

One bulldozer mounts another in an empty lot
Subway cars crawling on the trestle unfold into moths
My toes recite
                    The Gray Credo

   We believe the prehistoric imagination
was immense and tender and gray
   We believe dinosaurs were smothered by
the stale purity of their imaginations
   We believe there was once a color like
gray but it wasn't very serious and escaped
into the wind
   We believe gray has come home to roost
over the abandoned sleep of the Bronx

FOUR POEMS

First Prize

20 dark and wonderful dreams about the ice people

Voice

Nightcloud with the moon behind her

Apparition
for Ezra Pound

Petals on a wetback's brow

Prosody

Put the cop back on the beat

BOREDOM

for Ron Padgett

The sun folds with a royal flush
over the factory and the night shift
drops the deck and returns to work.
The building is immense and rectangular,
made of concrete blocks painted white outside
and gray within. The windows are large
but can't be looked through because they
are on the roof, to maximize the amount
of sunlight let in and minimize the cost
of electricity. When the workmen enter
the factory, they insert their time-cards
in the time-clock and go to their lockers.
They all wear gray overalls and paper hats.
This is the compulsory attire and the hats
are the butt of an inexhaustible joke: if one
worker passes another as they push
their carts down the aisle, he'll say:
"Hey, keep your hat on!"
They stack the boxes onto their carts
after removing them from the conveyor belts
and then wheel the carts out to the trucks and
freight cars parked in the rear of the buildings.
Like most factories, this one was built
in a location that affords an easy access
to railroad lines and interstate highways.
Let me think, has anything been left out?
Oh, yes, machines have been installed that dispense
coffee, cocoa, soup and crackers to the workmen.
Every man has his own locker. I already mentioned that.
But the overalls and hats are supplied without charge

and the laundry is also free.
Most of the men prefer to wear shoes with crepe soles.
Most of them drive to work in their own cars.
The foremen wear ties.
Everyone is overweight.
Production for the fiscal year that ended in April
would have exceeded all expectations
but no one had any.
Well, that does it.
I can't think of anything more to say.
It looks very tranquil here tonight.
The windows are glowing and the crickets
are, uh, what's the word for it, chirping?
The crickets are chirping in the grass
that grows along the chain-link fence
which surrounds this place. I don't know
if I've left anything out or not.
Maybe I should add that the factory may be burning.
Yes, I guess it is, it definitely is burning.
The warehouse is ablaze, that's for sure.
The flames are rather brilliant, more red than yellow,
but at this rate it's safe to say that they'll be
bright white in no time at all.
One of the warehouses is almost totally destroyed,
its steel frame is wavering in the intense flames.
Spectators have been gathering in the last few minutes.
A lot more are expected. It's going to be a long show.
Bleachers are in the process of being erected.
A few vendors are already selling refreshments.
There goes the steel frame I mentioned a few seconds ago.
Most of the refreshments are reasonably priced.
I don't recall seeing flames this tall before.

It's a veritable maelstrom, as they say.
A lot of folks came unprepared for this; walls
collapsing, roofs crumbling. Entire families
are sitting together in the bleachers,
mothers are trying to keep track of their children
and wipe the soot off their faces.
The havoc is undiminished.
It's hell out here all right.
The heat is causing some distress
among the less stalwart in the crowd.
The smoke is blacker than the late night sky,
it's billowing over our heads
dropping cinders onto people's laps.
I can see that some of the folks are getting
a bit fidgety. This is taking longer
than one would suppose. It's almost midnight
and this inferno has shown no signs of abating.
The firemen, I might add, though exhausted by now,
have not slackened their efforts in the least.
Chief Herlighy has issued a statement: he says
due to the intense winds and lack of equipment
it'll be quite a while before this fire ends.
The steel structures of the buildings are all
twisted like the pretzels that are being peddled
here tonight at a quarter apiece, the hoses
are leaping over the ground like spastic spaghetti
and, yes, there have been casualties: one
hook and ladder man has been undone by fatigue.
The flames are what can only be described as
spectacular. Some of the spectators are beginning
to leave. There's no chance of rain.
This fire will be burning for quite a while.

I can see a pinochle game or two in progress
and a few enterprising young couples
are playing volley ball behind the bleachers.
There's no lighting problem here.
Word has reached me that the police have gone home.
The wind has stopped but the fire certainly hasn't.
A lot of us are getting disgusted with all this.
Leaking hoses have turned this place into a swamp.
The remaining onlookers will have a hard time
getting away. Chief (what's his name, O'Herlihy?)
Chief O'Herlihy has said whatever water
is getting through the nozzles
evaporates before it reaches the flames.
He's afraid this one will just have to burn itself out.
His men are weary and bedraggled
but, he reminds us, fire fighters, no matter
how dedicated they are, can't subsist on cold coffee.
He also complains that this is the worst crowd
he's had to contend with in his 40 years as a fireman.
His men, he says, could have done a better job
if they weren't harassed by nosy spectators
but it's too late now and, as he puts it,
there's no sense crying over spilt milk...

ALBA

The train departs, lurching, locomotive
spewing smoke and sparks into the night
like a whale having a bad dream.

Starry morning

though the station platform always looks damp.
Milkweed growing through the slots
between the planks, pods unsealed
bright and silky.

Cross the tracks,
down the gravel slope and over the fence:

White sea, straw sea

the snow that froze smooth
over the field melted
months ago but the long grass
still bent in waves

birds sleeping in the empty waves

your absence crowded with thoughts of you

Harmatan

Nigeria
December 1966 – June 1967

1

Yesterday also has its leaves, newspapers
blown down the bare avenues
and streets of yet another city
entering the wide morning behind you, surprising
you that this light, often unnoticeable breeze
which constantly blows in your face
which carries sights through your eyes
like leaves through air,
can move these cities further away
than islands driven by an ocean stream
until all the buildings pale
and you can no longer hear the wooden bells,
the cats wailing in desolate markets
nor the soft grinding sound
of waves the large women made
scrubbing stone staircases
that spiraled up to a multitude of rooms.

4

Harmatan: monthlong winds off the Sahara.
Tents taut, straining.
In the morning, the sky's brown.
Step outside and vultures scatter
from the pots and bowls
except one that drags himself away, ragged
feathers hanging in a singed cape
scraping the soil behind him.
Edges worn off old mud houses.
Mice have eaten the corners off a book;
a round copy of Hazlitt's criticism.
Warped rulers, clocks clogged with sand.
To discourage thieves, the wall
circling the compound frosted with broken bottles
buried neck-down along the top
and now smoothed as glass found on a beach.
One at a time, at twilight, the vultures return
swooping on this leafless white tree
until there are so many
you can't see the branches.

8

Delirium. Malaria. Your mind tries
to escape its teeming shadow.
Sights lit by black lightning.
At daybreak, drained by the shivering
that shook you off the bed,
wander out into the fields,
not sure where the limits are,
where a life begins or ends.
Fields burned a week or two ago;
the villagers burn them before planting.
Wild flowers already sprouting
yellow, star-like in the black grass;
refuge in their scented light.
Have a cigarette,
welcome yourself back.
Strike a match,
hand shaky with a strange gentleness.
One star in the sky like an imagined one,
a faltering star that has seen
beyond its own light for the first time.

10

Tents pitched in a mango grove.
Bickering cooks.
Strong box chained
to one of the cots and poles.
The administrator from Sokoto
assigned the unmapped areas,
distributed aerial survey photos
and drove off with his catamite.
Somebody should tell the watchman
he doesn't have to heave bricks
to disperse the crowds
that come around to stare;
the mute, surpliced choir
at every campsite; the traders
displaying their jewelry,
flyswatters and red leather satchels,
wiping Kiwi shoe polish
on their ebony statues;
the students anxious to speak English.
Makeshift fence around the latrine.
Lanterns primed.
Cold whitemen slumped in canvas chairs,
writing, reading, stoking the fire;
and in the fading day, the dusty tantrum,
the wind trying to grab the light
and falling back on the unplanted ground.
Beethoven has replaced the Stones
on the portable record player,
batteries running low as the sun sets.
Solitary rider in black and gold cape.
Caparisoned stallion
prancing across the soccer field.

11

Another invitation from the emir
to come over for a few beers
at ten in the morning.
Kerchiefs, embroidered caps
blown high above the street.
Undecorated calabash stacked
next to dented, white Mercedes
at the entrance to his compound.
And what looks like a Savonarola chair.
Workmen have just finished repairing the wall
and stand before it, drawing
imbricated rows of arcs
across the still wet mud
with their outstretched fingers; a pattern
of grooves to ward off sun and wind.
This old village should move away from itself,
he says, a mile or two down the road
away from the sewage which has permeated
its foundations. Tribal scars
lost in his wrinkled face, his village
dying since the new highway bypassed it,
young people leaving for the cities,
the European doctors unable to cure him,
his oldest son a pompous dolt.
Tell me, are American albinos
whiter than our albinos?
Lukewarm beer out of the bottle.
Flies.
Boys with shaved heads.
The village scribe will help correct
any misspellings on the new maps.
Why don't you carry a rifle

or at least a pistol
when you go into the bush alone?
Your noisy bike won't frighten a boar
or a bush cow and there are places
you can only get to on horseback.

17

An oven made by packing mud
around discarded fuel drums.
A tongue for breakfast.
Unsliced, lying in the tin bowl
as if it had just pronounced its last syllable.
Three dried eggs. Powdered milk. Coffee.
By the third cup and cigarette, the metallic
sound of shaking leaves that hadn't felt rain
in months, herdsmen in the distance
running behind their flocks.
Thunderheads, black and purple, charging fast
over the horizon, wind sweeping the rain
ahead of them and dust clouds flying
up into the sky like a wish
to join the wind and be taken to the sea.
Jumped on the cycle and drove into it,
grass flattened as if by a wave,
ground turning instantly to mud
which spewed in a rooster tail off the rear wheel
and when blinded by the rain
you turned and raced the clouds back
to the mountain, the rocks, and nearing it
the lightning struck just then
a soundless white burst of time
into which everything vanished but you.

22

This bar in Malamfashi that sold cold beer.
Few sullen girls in the courtyard
and the owner, a big woman with a gold tooth
or two, a necklace of monkey paws
and skin like blue coal, aglow with the dye
that rubbed off her robe.
Circling the tables, collecting green bottles,
she finds a full one, brings it over
and takes the first swig:
"Deluxe," she confirms, "certifiably deluxe!"
Tuaregs wear robes like hers, buy them
in Kano, in a lot pitted with small craters
brimming with the dye; the heavy cloth dipped,
stirred, soaked, rinsed and pounded with mallets
till they're dry and stiff with a faint, uneven sheen.
You trip over hers on the way
to her room. A low, unlighted arcade.
"Duplex," she says, unlocking the door, "duplex!"
Her pet rabbits' cool, quivering noses
inspecting your ankles when you enter
and they jump in bed when she does,
hopping over your neck and back,
sweat wiped off on their white fur.
Robe on the floor. Dark smudges that rubbed off
on your skin. Shadows across the beams
and thatched ceiling. Rabbit asleep on your chest.
Trip over the night watchman on the way out,
who still refuses to wake up
when you start the bike.
Daylight seeping through the trees.

Cameo vultures walking on the road;
vultures will eat so much they get too heavy
to fly, to move out of the way
of the motorcycle
. . .feathers in your spokes.

24

Lebanese merchant guzzles an orange soda.
Two policemen in sharply creased blouses
and shorts pedal back to Katsina.
Hazy, windless acres.
Vultures, hundreds of them, descend
to forage among the locked stalls
and lean-to's and mount
the swept-up piles of scrap.
Momo quotes Plutarch:
People once believed the bird came
full grown from some other world
because a fledgling vulture was seldom seen.
And Hercules always considered
seeing one before an important event
a lucky omen because they were good-natured
creatures, they never damaged fruit trees
or corn or preyed on any living thing
and never touched another bird
even if it were dead.
He raises the volume of his new transistor
when he sees her: a Fulani girl
with hair braided into long, thin loops
and ankles steeped in metal bracelets,
totes a stack of unsold calabash bowls
out of the marketplace; sweat
trickling between her small breasts.
An older, snaggle-toothed girl
with mesmerizing eyes and a baby slung
in the robe around her waist
approaches her and they begin reciting

the standard greetings
before they're twenty feet apart:
How're your cattle, how're you, your father,
your mother, your brothers and sisters,
your sister's husband, your mother's sisters,
your mother's sisters' husbands . . .
and without breaking stride
they pass each other
still going down the list
even when out of earshot.

25

Pass the boulders where a family
of baboons had been earlier today.
Huge, muscular backs, grim faces
slowly turning to look at
you slowly backing away.
Tonight the sand is snow-bright.
No time to have put the muffler
back on the bike. A few lanterns on
at the mission. Watchman asleep
across the doorway of the main building.
No sooner does the nun hear
that Randy's temperature is 105
and climbing than she's grabbed her satchel
and hopped on the bike.
Holding on with one arm,
warning the short cut isn't a good idea.
Her white robes flying in the moonlight
and then later dissolving in the bushes
when she had to go ahead on foot.
Both tires flat, riddled by thorns.

28

Shaved heads passing through quiet alleys.
Men crammed in the backs of open trucks,
hands shielding their eyes.
Bala and Yusufu, in heavy woolen caps
pulled over their ears,
quit mending the tents to eat lunch.
Momo, the brim of his digger hat pinned up
with a brass insignia, advises you
not to share the meal because a gentleman
shouldn't mingle with laborers.
An angry youth with a Dutch fisherman's cap
pulled low over one vacant, bulging eye
disrupts a conversation
by accusing you of being a spy.
Palm wine—bought from a lanky old man
under a straw parasol of a hat—tastes vile,
almost too thick to drink.
Swallow it anyway, smoke some India hemp,
end up drawing on the plaster wall:
a wildebeest mounting a girl
wearing a striped kerchief.
Can't erase it all in the morning
before Ali the cook arrives with a new hula
that Ali the night watchman knitted for him.
One village on this section's map
is nameless since everyone there
thought you were a game warden
when you rode into it and ran away,
not stopping to retrieve the white caps
that fell off as you chased them

through the woods; not about to ride
fifty miles back there either;
but your sister's name sounds authentic,
it's her birthday
so name the place after her.

30

The sticks, so they burn slowly,
placed like spokes in the sand;
just the tips smoldering in the center.
No work today.
Can't see farther than fifty feet.
Sun a silver smudge.
A nudge of cows,
piebald goats hung like ornaments
in the dense gray air.
Wonder what color the sky will be tomorrow.
Sleepy eyes focusing on the short flame.
Mumble good mornings into a coffee cup.
Men clutching blankets
step squinting out of the tents
onto the decks of fogbound ships.
The young girl stoops, two big men
hoist the jug from under the spigot
and put it on her head;
erect, eyes gliming from its weight,
she turns and walks off
or fades, ascendant, into the ashen day.
Sounds from the village: women
pounding corn, husking peanuts.
Mice have gnawed the erasers
off every pencil.
Ibrahim thinks it a luxurious habit,
the way you just write on one side of a page.
He can't figure out
what you're doing here anyway
when you could be in America
making $540,000 a year.

33

Walk back to the bike:
front wheel wedged in a rotten stump
that was hidden by the tall grass.
A few loose spokes. Clean out the filter.
Jaw bone of an ass on the ground.
Slip it in the brake cables on the handlebar.
Get moving again, breeze
blowing the flies off your scraped knees;
gold, flowing grass and clear sky
coaxing your eyes away from the path again.
Then a distant cloud of dust to the right
and another to the left, moving in,
dogs, two packs converging in a cloud,
leaping over the handlebars,
all fangs and spit flying in strands;
grab the bone and swing,
crack it across their snouts,
batting wildly, snarls and whimpers.
Kick the bike into first,
pop the clutch, noise scaring them,
dance with it in neutral, pop it back,
rear wheel shooting sand into their eyes,
make it somehow to harder ground,
a little traction . . .
in the clear.
All their tails had a white tip.
Alarm still ringing in your head.
Thumbs blistered, ribs sore,
sound of the motor soon absorbed
in the silence again. Scraggy groves.

Huts grouped at the base of a hill
inside a matted fence. One mud house, new
with a checkered, whitewashed wall.
A little kid turns a corner and looks up,
drops a water jar from his head,
bursts out in tears and runs off.
First whiteman he'd ever seen.

35

The first time someone told it
(at the club bar in Zaria)
a man found a green mamba
curled around the handlebars of his BMW
just after he turned on the ignition.
In the second version, a couple
saw the snake in the same position
while driving home from Salah celebrations.
(Tight spot, what.)
In the third version, a man, considerably drunk,
looked down at his handlebars
and jumped off the bike
while going fifty miles per hour.
Stories drifting into the stale smoke
above the snooker tables.
Trophies. Dartboards. Gin and tonic.
Bingo once a week on the club patio
and old films from the States.
And then there's the one
about that trainload of Ibo refugees
that was doing all right
until it reached Tiv territory
where it was stopped and sent on
to Port Harcourt
with every passenger decapitated.
Loud, edgy Americans and boisterous Welshmen,
Nigerians with a penchant
for the words fuck and bloody,
German engineers and mechanics, Indians
and obsequious Indians.
A dreary English menu.
A blonde floating in a blue pool.

36

Peddlers with candy and cigarettes
on candle-lit trays
stroll through the rows of scooters
and bikes outside the open-air theatre.
Inside, young men, many of them with long,
manicured nails on their pinkies
to advertise the fact
that they don't work with their hands,
talk incessantly to their dates
while the three-hour film, made in Bombay,
ends with the squat hero
and pudgy, pouting heroine
ardently singing a duet for ten minutes
as they slide side by side
down a mountain of snow on their chests.
Crazed bugs in the projector's beam.
Subtitles unreadable in the fake, glaring snow
but by the time they reach the bottom
of the mountain they're obviously reconciled
and would embrace
if the Indian censors had allowed it.
A switch thrown a second too soon,
the final crescendo smeared
across the blank screen.
The audience rises, sandals peeling
off the sticky floor with their first steps.

43

Green light of a full moon.
Sokoto to Kano to the Jos Plateau,
wind stretching your face, bike roaring,
tracing roads between city lights
afloat in the darkness, lights
of a constellation that will finally end
when you follow time past it,
out of its midst, to some distant village
where maybe a language is spoken
that uses the same word for a well
as for a woman's eyes, for clarity
drawn from darkness, song from thought;
gravel splattered from the wheels
of oncoming trucks, lopsided, loaded
with bales of cotton, sacks of peanuts;
dragon-like, the headlight beams,
the smoky grinning grills;
taking curves at higher speeds
you widen an edge
that was no thicker than your shadow.
Instant dawn:
the day opens its red gate.
Night and day, which chases which?
A seclusion in speed,
the silence of heights from where you watched
clouds race their shadows to the shore,
cloud raining on its shadow,
rain falling white in the sunshine.

48

Somewhere the rivers are slowing down,
are less and less deep every year
and will soon be shallow enough to lie on
and let the water pour over you as you sleep;
the birds don't panic at dawn
and walk more than they fly; the ocean
sends one less wave ashore every day,
one more thought of sleep.
Fine dust above the goat paths
suspended in the sunlight
then drifting upward
as though the ground were raining on the sky.
The network of goat paths lining the ridges
and mounds which were once the city walls of Kano.
Sunlight, the memory of it, entering
the arid space of a demolished building in New York.
Dreamy movements of light and dust.
A slow shadow revolving at the center
of flattened miles,
one ant dancing with a dead ant in the sand.

Splurge

ONE FOR THE MONK OF MONTAUDON

I like to wake up somewhere
between Hawaiian music and Mormon architecture,
say, another coffee shop above the sea,
a silver, streamlined diner in the dawn
with chrome stools, cushioned booths,
cold food on a hot plate.

When the smoke clears,
I like to just continue,
sit on a brilliant windowsill
and enjoy the view; wonder about things
such as what's in it that makes glass
cast more of a shadow than some people I know.

I like to order another cup of coffee,
light another cigarette and admire the paint job,
check out the insects sealed under a third coat,
or see yet another sullen short order cook
bitch and grumble above the grill.

I love the way the waitress
can chew gum and sing while she wipes
the dust off a plastic plant
and then stop and talk about the weather.
And I love the dramatic weather:
the way the air changes with us,
the way another world arrives
in an avalanche of clouds,
the way the continents meet and separate again
while I jot down my immediate impressions
on a sheet of yellow paper;
taking note of little things, like the scorpion,

the first creature to walk on land;
or craters of illusion, great assumptions of normalcy,
where Ohio once was, or never was.

And I'm glad of a chance to meet people,
like Miss Ohio
("five foot nine, eyes that shine"),
if for no other reason than the pleasure
of shaking hands or the opportunity
of leaning into the distances
while a strand of smoke lingers, and rises,
and turns like an unheard but legible desire.

And the sight of a cat, undisturbed,
curled in the sunlight, pleases me;
or ketchup smears on table mats
of Venezuela and its hideous flowers;
or the sight of boys splattering peaches
against an ancient stone wall.

I just like to sit back and take it all in,
watch the sea and sky move together
like memory and imagination,
move me out of a dripping indolence
to a dripping cathedral, like Chartres
("walls of glass, roof of stone"),
where I can stand outside, see
whatever a summer sky can do, doing it all at once:
sunbursts through the daylong overcast
just when the rain begins to fall,
wind that leaps through the light and dark
to tear newspapers out of old grumps' hands

and raise the skirts of secretaries
who run by in groups that sound full of birdcalls
and smell like groves in bloom.

Or I just enjoy relaxing, follow
my thoughts and shadows
through the light of a vacant lot
where a cathedral once stood, or a cleaning store
("Clothes Cleaned In An Hour, Fresh As A Flower"),
and watch a cassowary stamp and scratch in the rubble,
able to explain the dust of his resentment
to anyone who might ask: although
he's not the only bird that can't fly, he is the only one
that can cripple a man with one swell foop.

And after the dust settles and the snow falls,
I like to listen to the cars
stuck throughout the hills,
tires that spin and smoke and wail,
attracting greater creatures
whose wings creak with sadness,
whose eyes sway with the stars.

And I like to sink into the bright desolation,
the sword-of-the-Lord glare
of empty, limitless parking lots,
the vast western skies above highways,
galactic pinball nights
when the wind carries my sight
and I'm lulled by the sound of passing trucks,
the surf-like rumble
that splashes a dusty light over my face.

Highway jetsam: hubcaps, tailpipes, a shoe,
mere logic's gleam in an empty bottle,
the spark of omniscience on my fingertips
wondering where the ocean went
that bared these gray miles, this unfinished world
where a miniature figure waves an armless sleeve,
greetings from the phantom of an ever-widening hour,
where fountains in the rain,
half frozen, half music,
shine with a dim dream of the sun.

Or after drinking white wine on a gray day,
I want to step outside,
see the rain fall with the snow
and lick it off my lips.
Another fast walker in the smeared city,
people huddled under umbrellas
like clumps of black mushrooms on the corners,
shriveled rainbows on the oil-stained sidewalk,
cars sprouting clear wings
as they cut through flooded streets.

And it's a good day
when the wind is pure sensation
and I can lie in the garden with my lady,
watch the crows slide sideways above the clearing
and squirrels trash through the treetops;
when I can listen to dragonflies
roll in a dogfight over the snowpeas
and the wind fizz through blighted pines;
or watch my shadow climb after a yellow bird
through the towering ruins of memory.

And by the rings of St. Elmo,
it's a good day when I can stretch out
under the magnolia tree,
hear its limbs rub the ground,
see its flowers still filled with water
days after it's rained.
In a place like that I like to think
about where I've been
—Milwaukee, Cleveland, Dallas—
or where I'm not sure I've been
—Milwaukee, Detroit, Tenerife—
Just put a shining finger on the globe
and cloud-crawl above the spin,
from Agadir to Inertia.
An occasional pastime,
and the past is endless:
Hausaland to Sokoto, Senegambia
to Isfahan, Kabul, Baluchistan,
the Southern Limit of the Grain,
the Southern Limit of the Vine,
the Standing Bear, the Gold Flies,
the Blue-eyed Dog, Yenner's Slopshop,
muezzins' voices and kites
whirling above the skyline,
craven runts suddenly dancing through trashfires
on a hilltop intersection,
or jumping through stars reflected in the Bosphorus.
Dutch junkie in a sweetshop
slouched over the jukebox;
just me and a few shivering cheerleaders
loitering in Asia Minor.

On a good day, I'm glad I was there
and glad I'm not there now,
another paleface in the middle of winter
living on hotel roofs covered with plastic,
almost asleep beside the trashfire
while French tramps broadjumped the flames.

Sparks and singed hair.
Moonhole through a dome of clouds
or starlight through plastic,
withered plastic flapping above the heat.
Cold, thick fingers. Mine.
And I could see myself in time
the way the log burned brighter than the flames.
The years below, rooms
with the furniture removed,
where moths rested on my bare arms
and spiders descended into conversations
on spectral parachutes;
where the words flowed
and the beginnings of all my thoughts
sat behind me like an idol in the night,
the dark and fearsome generosity,
the eyes of some gigantic child
who has never spoken, never slept.

And I swear by the Blue Saint of Tolerance
that when the future looks bright
I'm as happy as a flame in a lumberyard,
and nothing pleases me more
than to sit under a clear sky
at a table piled high

with oysters and shrimp, mushrooms and veal,
wine, strawberries, brandy, coffee and mints.
For it's a pure and simple joy
to eat and drink with those I love,
to stay late and celebrate
a few certainties
while confusion and scorn
and a few other crazy, weather-beaten guests
continue to roll across the cold floors,
out the doors, the gates, the empty palace of the night.

And I like the sweet, weary feeling
of going sleepless, aimless through city streets,
have the action and ebullient tones
carry me like the first wave-borne beer can
to near a pristine shore;
and then wallow in the sunlight
as the day drifts into one long morning,
sit on a bench and gaze at the river
and, above its glimmer of forgetfulness,
at the wild blue yonder,
and wonder whether the haze between
—like a life—joins or separates them.

I like to consider what else
could be more important than kindness and work,
or think of a better way to end a day
than to lie on a lawn
as the sun casts a net of shadows
below the leafless trees, a net
that slides over me and gathers in its gentleness
what a mind finds too heavy to force away.

And for a while I am outside of time,
amazed by what's left of me
and all there is to know.
I can close my eyes and bask in a satisfaction
that begins to glow with silence;
it could be green, dark green, the entrance
to the deep, empty well
that Pliny told astronomers was the best place
from which to watch stars move in daylight.
And though he meant that as practical advice,
it sounds to me like a prayer
from one of those barren, cloudy lands
that I've seen and liked,
forgotten and then wrote about.

TRIPTYCH

MORNING

6:30 (2) Sunrise
     (4) Knowledge
     (5) Comparative Geography
   (13) Images and Things
   (71) Listen and Learn
7:00 (2) News
     (4) News
     (5) WIDE WORLD
     (8) Public Affairs
7:30 (4) Young Africans
     (9) Elsie Aquacade
   (10) The Young and the Restless
   (13) Religious Humoresque
   (71) Espionage
8:00 (2) Asian Dimension
     (5) To Be Announced
     (6) Vanishing Point. A Sentinel in Swamplight; snow falling on black mud.
   (10) WEATHER. Flood footage, birds hop from branch to branch as the water rises higher and higher.
8:30 (8) PERIPLUM
     (9) Mr. Itchy Starlight
   (11) DUENDE. He drives into a tree, he listens to the apples bounce off the hood of his car.
8:45 (9) WEATHER. Thunderclaps, the clouds stampede.
   (10) SUBMISSION
9:00 (2) Bugs Bunny
     (7) Snorkeling with Captain Bravo.

     (8) TALES. "Why all this fear and trembling?" said the Wizard to the Shrew. "Is life all you know?"
9:30 (80) Violence in Blue
     (4) Lisping Marauder
   (71) El Reporter
10:00 (7) SERMON. What part of paradise is made of memory?
     (9) SCIENCE. A hammock rope is tied around a tree; as the trunk grows the bark swallows the rope and leaves an interesting scar.
10:30 (13) MODERN EXPLORATION. The space a seemingly mindless, rush hour crowd leaves around a raving idiot.
   (71) BLINDSPOT
11:00 (2) FANFARE. Blood on a concrete piano.
     (4) LOVELORN. Figure on a mountaintop digging up seashells.
     (5) Dragonquest.
     (7) Elizabethan and Nova Scotian Music (with Charles North).
11:30 (9) FEATURE. Telling fortunes by burning seaweed.
   (13) MUTINY. Fog drifts up to the house and crashes through the windows. Elephants bark in the distance.
   (71) FUTURAMA

12:00 (4) News
(7) News and Weather.
The wind hunting
silence.
(8) INQUISITION
12:30 (2) A CHILLING TALE.
A man with long
blonde hair hands a
threatening note to a
teller with long
blonde hair.
(13) MODERN EXPLO-
RATION. A deer
trying to climb
a ladder.
(71) NECROPOLIS
(6) INTERLUDE.
Poisoned rats rot in
the walls. You
vacuum large black
flies off the screens.
1:00 (5) WHITE STRAWBERRIES
(7) SNORT. No war
buff, me.
(8) Damaged Perspective
(9) APPLIANCES AT
AN EXPOSITION
(10) Smut
1:30 (6) TIME SPAN. ". . .
and the spiders were
singing in the wells."
(71) SCIENCE. An examination
into the earwax of various
races. Curious results.
(80) WEATHER. Bleak
snowlight, black helicopters
to the rescue.

1:45 (4) Dream Overload
(5) A Stack of Bibles
2:00 (2) VIGIL. 8 people on
a train platform
reading little books.
(4) DISCOVERY. My
elbow, the left one,
the first time I've
noticed it in years.
Highlights: scars
from unremembered
wounds, new hair.
(5) Polyphemus
(13) LA HISTORIA. The
men in Columbus'
crew are allotted over
two liters of red wine
per diem.
2:30 (6) Mostly Prose. A bug
flies through my eye.
The crowd cheers.
(8) CHERISHED
FORMS
3:00 (7) Conquistador
(13) MODERN EXPLO-
RATION. Spaces in
the air where the
wind waits disguised
as silence.
4:00 (4) JUMPING JESUS
(5) Split Second
4:30 (6) VANISHING
POINT. And I sink
through the chilly
rain and leafless
trees, past the color-
ful clothes left out on
the line.
(8) SPORTS AND
WEATHER. Click,

clunk. People bowling
in the fog.

5:00 (2) HOMILY. A long
lost color returns to
earth in a fleet of
clouds, ending millennia
of heretofore
inexplicable melancholia.

(9) BITCH ON WHEELS

6:00 (2) Hitleresque

(13) ARCHAEOLOGY.
Pillars strewn wowie-
zowie across the sea
floor of a sunken
palladium.

(71) RALPH WONDERFUL

(80) Bucharest

7:00 (2) News

(4) Cow with a hair-lip:
Moof.

(7) NEWS AND WEATHER.
Intermittent gales
which drown the
crickets, hundreds of
acorns hit the roof
and roll down the
shingles.

EVENING

7:30 (13) Brahms. Piano
Concerto #2 in B flat
major.

(45) Pythagoras

8:00 (2) UPDATE. The
magicians explain
why they failed.

(9) SOUVENIR. A

pubic hair, a perfect
6, on a bar of soap.

9:00 (7) ART which was not
interested in motion
or time.

(9) HOUR OF BLISS

(11) STRANGE ENCOUNTER.
"Neither darkness
nor light," said the
Swamp Angel,
"Neither darkness
nor light can fill my
eyes."

10:00 (2) CUISINE. Does torn
bread really taste better
than sliced bread?

(8) Black Dimes

10:30 (7) MY BLOOD RAN COLD

(9) The Young Elpenor.
Besotted, he falls off
roof, breaks neck,
dies. The sea-dark wine.

(11) KARMA. The live
leafless branches and
the dead tree against
the sky, all grappling
with the wind.

(71) TIME AND TOLERANCE.
An invisible nude enters
the elevator. She's
chewing gum.

11:00 (2) Moon out of focus

(5) INTERMISSION.
She leaves the table,
her elbows are wet.

(6) Cloud Armada

(8) Hours bubbling in
the everlasting wake
of paradise.

(11) CANYON. Another

herd faceless and innumerable rushes by without showing Biff and Sally the way out.

11:30 (5) WAVES wearing war bonnets charge a pair of plump identical twins.

(6) FIFI FLEES—FOUL PLAY FEARED.

(8) TYPICAL BAUDELAIRE. "...no point is sharper than that of the infinite."

12:00 (2) LUMINARY. In 1903, he turned his attention to the East...

(9) WATERLOO. Napoleon loses because severe case of hemorrhoids prevents him from concentrating on the course of the battle.

(11) FINISHING TOUCHES. A cloud floats up to the moon and stops. Jolting finale avoided.

PROBE AND BROOD

The one meal so far
blown away
before anyone could take a bite
the sea jumping through the cargo hatch
slamming everything
benches people tin plates
back against the bulkhead

Lie in a sea of hammocks
and listen to my hair grow
Polyglot steerage
Slumped Africans
blowing dope at the gray ceiling
puking on the gray deck

This hammock my own wave
from The Gambia to Las Palmas
        (Or maybe it was
        Las Palmas to Cadiz)

Sun high off the stern
Deckhands heave garbage
to the sharks

Yawn and stare into the wake
the commotion
the past being cut loose

Rainbow in the spray

Waves slip through foam
sharks through waves
hearts through sleep

UPSTATE

"Steepletop," Austerlitz, New York home of
/   - -   /   -   - /
Edna St. Vincent Millay

located west of a hill
where we often camped
(once in ten-below weather)
and just above Stone's Garage
(where we went to get warm
in the winter, cokes in the summer)

A big laconic man with one ear missing
Stone collected antique cars
When he did speak this fly would
              dart out of the black holᵉ

                                        in
                                      he
                                      t

                              side

                                of
                             his
                  head

and then climb back in
when he stopped

And customers would sit there
and listen and try not to watch

OUTSIDE BABY MOON'S

The Kelly Square Smoke Shop closes its doors,
a porter empties the ashtrays
in the lobby of the Gold Tooth Hotel, a grate is drawn
over the Wonderhorse Bar and Grill.
The last van has entered the garage
of the Reliable Music Factory,
the plug's been pulled on the jukebox at Baby Moon's.
Someone sweeps the aisles
of the Fluxus Total Impact and Window Cleaning Company,
the Rainbow Caste Systems and Storage Concern is dark,
members of the House of the Intimate Ultimate
have sung their last hymn.
The tower next to Sleazy Victor's
and the Cougar Belch Correspondent School
looms blacker than the night sky
and a neon fixture flickers in a showcase
at the Admirable Admiral Demolition Project.
Only the sign on the Soft Dart Prelude
remains lit, the Stardust Furniture Exchange
and the Frost Collision Works are deserted.
In just a few more hours, the first customers
of the day will enter the Kelly Square Smoke Shop,
shades will rise on the windows
in the Gold Tooth Hotel, a fleet of vans
will pull into the Reliable Music Factory.
Long fluorescent tubes in the Rainbow Caste Systems
and Storage Concern will soon be switched on
and secretaries will be madly typing away
under Sleazy Victor's vacant eyes.
Old men will unfold crisp newspapers
at the Frost Collision Works
and blueprints will be re-examined

at the Admirable Admiral Demolition Project.
Toes will be tapping at the Soft Dart Prelude,
wide-eyed, winsome girls will be dancing
on the roof of Baby Moon's, but you,
Faithless Reader, you'll still feel like a leaf
lost in a pile of gloves.

RIFACIMENTO

cinema—an Asian girl with an African name
torpor—the fate of mastodons
bandito—a minor bandage
scoundrel—a French goblet for special occasions
Monotony—when capitalized, an extinct South Seas god
plenitude—where albatross prefer to land
Anglo-Saxon—a frenetic dance of the Twenties
endow—to retrieve an ear
sponsor—a musical insecticide
tin—an epicene curse
Betty—at 3 o'clock, unfriendly aircraft
metaphors—I use them. They keep me regular.
Peloponnesian—being licked by an azure tongue
Rasputin—Oh, I was just rasputing around, trimming the Peenemunde.
Cro-Magnon—You dial your own number; you get a busy signal.
anaconda—dry thunder
vehemence—paper that butchers use for wrapping veal
sociable—looking at a battleship through a keyhole
Transvaal—running up a flight of stairs with an erection
cotillion—running down a flight of stairs with an erection

SNOWBLIND TO BANQUET

Snowblind, bats chased out of a cave into the dazzling day. I've kissed my vocabulary goodbye. A little leg room a little ventilation, I'll be all right as soon as I scrub these red eagles off the walls and have a cup of espresso. This place has the stale aura of an exiled journalist reading soggy newspapers by moonlight: pages noiselessly torn as they're turned, pictures of motorcades and visiting dignitaries, boom towns, ghost towns, and more visiting dignitaries. But from now on it's going to be all swaying trumpets and smoking clarinets, semi-private melodies and women with different colored eyes. Jumping Jesus! Here comes Rabelais, and look at the words he's brought with him: here's "flake" and "shambling," here's "concupiscent" and "splurge," "camouflage," "concourse," and "banquet."

PHENAKISTES URGES HIS CREW ONWARD

To reject years of sporadic nihilism
(*nec* hope *nec* fear)
and then sail down the Nile itself
on a soggy, fly-blown raft, carried all the way
by the same wave; dreary days
beneath the taunts of snide cliff-dwellers,
rancorous-eyed vultures, dim-witted natives
pelting the slack sail with apple cores;
oars jammed in purple mud, stench of wet dogs
and the river fanning out finally to the sea:
a morning where it will be impossible
to prove or disprove anything, a sky
that retains the stars of the previous night
hours after the dark evaporates;
white stars above the sparkling sea,
dream-winged dragonflies gliding in the warm wind,
delta reeds vibrating, a-sway,
then the soundless, level end
—your masks burning to a glossy red ash,
shadows flowering into reflections...
Or to follow another route
perched on the edge of a glacier,
a frozen river that pushes the days
ahead of itself, to sit there
and maybe applaud as if it were a seat
in the front row of a new language
that was creating valleys, disrupting societies,
shoving them and their slot-eyed goats aside
in order to stay on the verge of a white flood
and despise all nostalgia except
the quintessential longing for another arctic,
crater-like stadium, islands

covered with lava, snow and steaming wells,
flames and ice prospering together,
a splendor brightened even more by a lunar envy,
the mornings red, the earth rounder
and the unobstructed call of voices
skidding for miles over the ice.

EXACTA

And they're off!

Babe Wittgenstein takes the lead

It's Babe Wittgenstein
Morbid Blonde
Queasy Phantom
Princess Spits
Squeaked Aorta
Dream Helmet
and Pigs in Moonlight

Princess Spits coming up fast

It's Babe Wittgenstein
Morbid Blonde
and Princess Spits
Babe Wittgenstein has the edge

Here comes Dream Helmet
neck and neck
with Queasy Phantom

Pigs in Moonlight losing ground
Princess Spits nosing out Babe Wittgenstein
They're bunched up on the rail
Queasy Phantom with blinkers on
It's Princess Spits by a length
Babe Wittgenstein and Morbid Blonde nose and nose

Rounding the turn
Dream Helmet on the outside

Squeaked Aorta out of the running
It's Princess Spits and Morbid Blonde
Babe Wittgenstein losing ground
Pigs in Moonlight breaking sharply
Queasy Phantom takes the turn

It's going to be close
It's Princess Spits Morbid Blonde
Babe Wittgenstein Dream Helmet
Queasy Phantom Pigs in Moonlight
and Squeaked Aorta trailing the field

A little daylight now
between Babe Wittgenstein
and Pigs in Moonlight

It's going to be tight
Princess Spits fighting it out
with Morbid Blonde

It's Princess Spits
It's Morbid Blonde
It's Princess Spits

Queasy Phantom slowing down
Dream Helmet two lengths behind
Pigs in Moonlight

They're going into the stretch

Morbid Blonde out front
Pigs in Moonlight closing fast

Here comes Pigs in Moonlight
sweeping past Princess Spits
Morbid Blonde and Pigs in Moonlight neck and neck
Babe Wittgenstein tiring falling back
It's Morbid Blonde
It's Pigs in Moonlight
It's going to be Pigs in Moonlight
Pigs in Moonlight has the field
Pigs in Moonlight charging through
It's Pigs in Moonlight
Pigs in Moonlight winning by two lengths

CHEESEBURGER SERENADE

with a side of French

Another glacier passed by last night,
scraped the paint
off the side of the house
and knocked over the garbage cans.
I write about it now
with a beautiful new pen, a gift,
a slim, steel-gray Astropoint®
that came with a lifetime guarantee.
The glacier was new, too.
The ice was clear as day
and inside it were a lot of familiar people.
I didn't know I disliked so many people.
But there they were,
fingers splayed, eyes wide open,
tongues stuck to the ice:
all the blithering sops
and penny-sucking nits,
and flunks and rank phonies,
the back-firing wimps
who used to wander around
like midgets in a pool hall,
the cheap chiselers who slid along
like snails on their own slime.
I should tell you more.
[*Aside: Il allait au nord.*]
I should tell you in glorious Latin.
I should commission the rug weavers of Tashkent
to spend the next decade
illustrating the scene with silk and spun gold!
But I am ashamed of my joy.

SNORKELING WITH CAPTAIN BRAVO

A belief in the perfectibility of man boodle loop bloodle loop bloop bloop bloop can only lead to despair and needlessly heavy breathing bloodle loo loo bloop bloop bloop try not to laugh bloodoop just keep those flippers working close to the surface sputter sputter between worlds goolp goolp the fatal yawn of totalitarian bloodle loop boodle loop the violent die stupid deaths bloop bloop avoid cults goolp no theory no bloop system no book will save you dooloop doop doop be a true seeker and fall forever upward like an angel bloop bloop bloop

ANATOLIA

for Ann

Snow falling on the desert, snow falling on the sea, wake up in between, wind filtered through bullet-riddled stop signs, taste the cold spoon of dawn, the crazy birds are jumping in their nests, your hair is my black moon, your lips touch my ears, breathe the sound of beautiful new cars speeding past me as I drive through Turkey again, only this time I know you're there too, though I don't know exactly where, town after town, wide muddy streets, icy wooden buildings, packs of horses and glum, sloppy soldiers, snow blown over windswept roads, revenant waves, and the veiled women walking through them, speechless, out of the white, glaring hills. I can hear my heart out there, footsteps across the frozen fields.

INDEX

Likewise

ABUNDANCE

In Brueghel's great picture *Canal Street*,
restaurant customers order roast swan
instead of chicken, hurled salad
instead of tossed salad, while shoppers
spill through a maze of stalled trucks
and scurry around the sidewalk stalls
jammed with countless nameless things
that housewives sidestep
to surround a Japanese man
in a broad-brim hat and painted silk tie
as he demonstrates how one gadget
can cut food fifty different ways
and though they don't understand a word
he says, they stand transfixed by his spiel
amid the fumes and noise and loud fruit vendors
dropping casual perfections of sun and rain
into bags and sacks against a backdrop
of silver towers and sea and fields
vibrant with excess that giddy farmers hail
by tossing animals, large animals,
into the air to be carried away
on the winds of exuberance
to the four corners of the globe
where the romping gods
bear so many attributes
they're a bundle of incongruities
and no one takes them seriously
not even their beaming angels
who parachute drunkenly down to the shore
distracting the dogs let loose on cormorants
that ate so much they can't fly
but not the boys in the rowboat

who have caught a blowfish,
tickled its belly until it's about to burst
like a balloon before dropping it overboard
to watch it blow itself backward to kingdom come,
nor the other children who have stopped
clamoring over the stranded whale's back
to swim out underwater, under the swans,
grab them by the legs and yank them down
in a slow fury of bubbles and light
and then sell them to the market
near the restaurant in the foreground
of Brueghel's great picture *Canal Street*.

PARKWAY

The night is nothing more than the night,
the moon little more than the moon.
But what better light to fill in the blanks
of a long conversation, the simple fact
of it filling those barren seas:
Sea of Clouds, Sea of Nectar, Sea of Dew.

Colors, too, and cold facts are enough,
the champions of a poem, a conversation,
whatever's on the move—a voice slow
and easy like chilled vodka.
Or, as Clarity said to me,
"Let's shoot the breeze.
The night is a little bluer than last night,
the moon a little more than full."

IN PRAISE OF IDLENESS

For the second time this week
I've watched snow fall at sunrise,
dawn arrive on a breeze
(the way I think it always does).
I don't know which, time or the weather,
woke me, charmed me out of a dream
where a few of us floated around,
gravity's jokers,
face-up in the quiet water
and the jetsam of a slow life.
I had one line that I'd saved
and let it go as though it were mine,
calling for "Darker days and brighter gods!"
Then I only had my waking instant,
but it opened with that same shadowless light,
a sense of change, of something both near
and remote, first and last,
blowing with the wind and snow
through my reflection in the window.
And then I lost it.

So here I am, with cigarettes and cold coffee,
an unfinished ode to idleness,
cobwebs in high places,
a spider that rappels down the bookshelves,
and a commotion recollected in tranquility;
sunlight pouring through,
and another bright page
with a peculiar darkness flowing over it
—shadows of heatwaves from the radiator,
or my thoughts going up in smoke.

The glass, when misted over,
reminds me of store windows,
how they're swathed with soap,
shrouded in secrecy
before a grand opening
or after an ignominious closing.
Either way, not very interesting
except, perhaps, when the graffiti,
the anonymous messages, appear
scrawled across them
by some child of the air,
words you can see through
or a clear smear.

And at twilight I'm still here,
the same place, the same light.
Nothing to do but move with the view:
snow, wind over soft ruins,
unfinished buildings that loom
like monuments to a spent curiosity.
I'm in the tallest, up here with the Nopes
roosting on soggy flunkgirders.
Want a cigarette? Nope.
Got a match? Nope.
See any alternative to solipsism? Nope.
Hedonism? Nope. Sloppy stoicism? Nope.
Did you know that Maryland
has no natural but only manmade lakes? Nope.

The creatures of idleness
are pure speculation.
They follow the weather,

shadow the wind, fill in the blanks.
Some are big and clumsy and sly
and like to lick my watch;
others, like gerunds,
have already drunk themselves
into a state of being.
Another, with time on his hands
and the sense of how windows
are both inside and outside a place,
stands there watching his silhouette
change to a reflection
as the light shifts
and he moves forward or back,
plays like a god
stepping in and out of himself,
and hears the wind as the breath of change
when the last flurry whirls away in the light.

The last flake grows larger
as it descends, and presents,
when it lands in a burst of brilliance,
the floorplan for a new building
where every wet, beaded window
is a picture of pleasure and expectation.
The drops ripen, moments in the light,
questions that, answered by a feeling,
slide away as clear as my being,
a drop at a time down the glass.
When the wind blows this hard
it's about to say something at last.
The earth down to its bare magic,
wind and glass, water and light.

TRIOLET

Wind and water, glass and light,
Send her what she needs,
A clear song on a quiet night.
Wind and water, glass and light,
Nothing else in sight,
No way to know where her heart leads.
Wind and water, glass and light,
Send her what she needs.

KING NASTY

"Let me sketch it out for you,
off the top of my head.
I'll tell you what I want,
you fill in the blanks.
Begin smack in the middle,
the French Revolution, the Reign of Terror,
the glub and gloom of disillusionment,
the mumbo jumbo of annihilation.
Let the gray sets
—sluggish music, sparse dialogue,
mostly grunts and noise—alternate
with the tumult of the daylight crowds,
the din, the frenzied color,
all bellow and froth.
Open with a long shot, Place de la Concorde.
Move in over the rooftops and skylights,
troops and proclamations.
Aim at the headsman.
He's at the pinnacle of his career,
trouncing around the scaffold,
ablaze with sunlight.
Make the scaffold about 100 square feet,
unseasoned wood.
Drop to the prisoner, a skinny runt
tied face-down to a plank.
The headsman looms over him,
the guillotine rig over the headsman.
His boots slip on the blood-soaked deck
as he shoves the runt onto the lock.
I want a high-angle shot of the blade,
silver, white, then pan left
until it's lost in the sun.
The blade drops, the crowd cheers.

Now, this executioner, he's big, right?
The crowd calls him Big Boy.
He wears a mask that flaps down
over his nose. Large eyeholes.
A black mask, and a leather apron,
beefy arms, hairy, a black tooth or two.
Floppy boots, you know the kind.
A scraggle-toothed lummox, but professional.
Give him a tattoo: a crown pierced by a dagger.
Did they wear tattoos then?
I think Cook's crew
had brought them back from Tahiti.
Check it out.
Whatever, make sure it's lurid.
You get the idea.

All right. It's noon. The chain rattles,
the blade rises: a slow crank.
Cut to quick shots of the next prisoners.
You ever read Byron's letters, the one
where he describes the executions he saw?
Well, that's what I want.
The first prisoner sobbing;
the second stunned, dumb;
the third sneering, scornful,
still trying to wrench free.
They bind the first to the plank,
lay him down, lock him in.
Another shot of the high rig,
the cross-piece, the blade.
Then its whispering fall
and—thud, the head drops, and bounces,
the legs twitch crazily.

No, wait! Scratch that. I got it.
While the blade rises and all that,
cut to the spectators:
old hags, young damsels, students,
business types, burghers—
you know, the usual crowd scene.
But catch these two fellows taking bets
on how many times the heads will bounce.
Then the thud, and a split-second shot
of the neck before it erupts.
A four-foot spray at least.
—Oh, hold it. The head has to bounce.
It bounces twice and rolls.
The loser in the crowd curses
and jabs a coin into his pal's palm.
Quick switch to the second prisoner.
His head bounces three times in a long shot.
Again the roaring multitude.
This time the guy wins the bet.

Now the third victim.
Follow Byron to the letter on this one.
A burly man, he struggles all the way.
Big Boy can't close the stock,
can't lock it over his thick neck.
He has to sit on it.
The victim keeps pulling back,
so when the blade hits, it takes off his head
just above the ears.
No spurt of blood this time,
just a slow white ooze.
And the top of his head shouldn't bounce,

just flop on the boards like a bowl.
The crowd boos Big Boy,
who is truly annoyed.
The bettors curse and call it a draw.
Through all this, work in a cameo:
The young Goethe, play him up with commentary,
the astute, disinterested observer.
Good chance for exposition here.
End the scene with his pronouncement
that the whole noisome show
displays "a stupidity that defeats the gods."
I also want to see somebody
retch into a silk handkerchief.
I've always wanted to see that.
And I want poetry in the dialogue,
at least two and a half heaves per line.

Next scene—Am I going too fast? —
Early morning dark, misty.
The same place, the plaza empty.
Move in on a few garbage men
working under the scaffold.
Did you see that film *Danton*?
Well, I didn't either,
but somebody told me about a shot in there
that I want you to copy.
Only make it original.
Two carts with high wooden wheels,
no spokes—or does that sound medieval?
I don't know. Check it out.
These garbage men, they're grim, they're stooped,
they have broad shovels

and they're scooping up the clotted blood
and straw under the platform,
and dumping it onto the carts.
This is a very quiet scene.
The blood is thick and black
and they walk and wobble on it
like Lilliputians on a plate of Jello.
Big Boy is working late.
He's talking to an officer.
Clandestine executions in the works.
They're discussing a new delivery,
prisoners packed into a tumbrel,
its wheel rims muffled,
wrapped in burlap.
The officer offers a bribe.
Big Boy resists, none of the prisoners
is on his list, the risk is great, et cetera.
The officer points to the moody goons
guarding the tumbrel
and Big Boy mulls it over and complies,
shoving the money under his apron.
Keep it realistic.
They should speak in French accents,
so give them a shot of Novocain in the lips.

Now, see if you can make this work.
The bribing avengers take over.
Torchlight and twisted faces.
No choreographed slaughter here
but the worst of it: hatred,
wild cruelty, sloppy horrors.
Get it? A little revolutionary excess.

I'll give you my notes on what happened
at Poitiers and Lyon
and the September Massacre.
Follow that scenario.
Have the goons and zealots
bugger the aristocrats
after they lock them in the guillotine.
Have them signal Big Boy to drop the blade
so the gagged and screeching aristos
die in a boing-eyed shudder
just as the buggers' frenzy peaks.
Don't overdo it.
Close the scene with something subtle,
artistically redeeming—say,
a wizened crone on the sidelines
quoting Montaigne.

After that, slowly back out of the set.
Mist again, the scaffold in lantern light,
then fog filling it all to a gray blank.
Hold it for a few seconds,
no image but the sound
of slow wings, gradual, heavy flight,
rhythmic, heaving the air aside.
But instead of wings it's a man's arms
swinging as he walks,
his sleeves brushing his coat,
hardly discernible, nearly disembodied.
Then his face—it's Big Boy sans mask,
heading home after a rough day.
Lead him down a side street.
Deep gutters, narrow, filthy, wet.

He opens a low door and enters
a smoky kitchen, dark, colorless.
His wife lugs a kettle to the stove,
pokes around the hearth.
She's glum, harried.
Three glum children, dirty, expressionless.
Big Boy hunches over the table,
thick fingers splayed on the rough boards.
A metal plate under his chin: stew.
Slobbering, he wipes up what's left
with a chunk of bread, wipes it clean
until there's a shadow,
the blur of his reflection on the plate.
—No, cancel that.
But I want a lot of weight.
I want the kitchen to be like a cave.
Everything quiet.
Even the smoke droops.
His wife plops a pair of boots in front of him.
He examines the soles, the new studs.
Now cut to a flashback at the plaza.
The usual faces, sunlight.
Prisoners jammed into a rickety tumbrel.
Right out of *A Tale of Two Cities*.
A dreary parade of tumbrels.
Close shots of the jeering uglies.
Contempt and boisterous condemnation.
Go for the strong contrast
with the prisoners' stupor.
Young, old, priests, poor folk,
gaunt aristocrats, baffled and weeping.
You know the bit: devastation and woe.

Then a quick series of beheadings:
Chop, chop, chop.
The ballooning shadow of Big Boy
on the smeared planks.
Even his shadow looks bloated.
His boots slip and he falls on his butt.
He's the entertainer, playing to the crowd.
The blood thick and thin, curdled and fresh.
Big Boy on tiptoe now.
He yanks a periwig off an aristo's head
and skims it over the waving spectators.
Now—no, hold it. Now I've got it!
One head rolls to his feet.
He looks down and he hears, he sees
the head say something!
The background noise is tremendous
but he's sure he's not deceiving himself.
The head makes a sound.
You've got to catch his incredulity.
Make sure the eyeholes
in the mask are large enough for that.
Hold the close-up.

Now a jump-cut back to the kitchen,
where he's at the table, slumped, sullen,
and remembering this as the wife
and children putter around.
This next shot is crucial:
One of the children is drawing on the wall.
She's using pairs of knots
in the wallboards for eyes.
The wasted Big Boy watches her

as she fashions, very delicately,
one face after another.
Another flashback:
Again he sees that head make a sound.
It's not a gurgle, not a gasp,
but a definite word.
Now keep cutting in
with a series of flashbacks,
at least five or six,
in which he recalls other heads
on other days, other victims
who also said something to him.
Cut to the mute child
outlining more faces in pencil.
The pairs of knots portray
every human expression
but mostly downcast, mostly dread.
A lot of faces! Make that wall
look like a whirlwind in the underworld
where nothing is left of the spooks
but their dark eyes, their feelings.
Then keep intercutting to the heads
that Big Boy has seen speak.
I need a big buildup here,
maybe something from Beethoven's *Eroica*,
as Big Boy, bristling with revelation,
realizes that all this time
the words that the heads have been uttering
are forming phrases. . .
and that the phrases are on their way
to a sentence . . .
Maybe run all the different heads by

in a montage first:
sweet, horrified, deadpan.
Give each a word as if they were
Burma Shave signs on the roadside
and Big Boy's waking up at the wheel.
First head: "It's . . ."
Second head: "when . . ."
Third: "men . . ."
Fourth: "try . . ."
Fifth: "to . . ."
Sixth: "be . . ."
Seventh: —Cut it off there for now.
Then have Big Boy hear them repeated—
"It's when men try to be . . ."
—by one voice that sounds
like the unimaginable, a cosmic echo,
a god's first scream of disbelief.
You know, lightning
and something else, something red, not thunder.

Yeah, it's far-fetched
but it'll work.
I got the idea from reading
about that German pirate, Stoertebaker.
When the British finally caught him,
before they cut off his head
they gave him a last request.
He said, "Kill me standing up
and spare as many of my crew
as I can run past after you swing the axe."
So, they cut off his head
and he manages to make it past fourteen of them.
What a class guy, a stand-up guy.

Anyway, back to Big Boy.
Jump ahead.
Multitude and spectacle.
Big Boy's back on the job.
He's slowed down, the pace with him.
He's not playing to the masses anymore,
he's more deliberate.
After each head drops, he stares at it,
waiting for the next word in the sentence.
No one else, none of his assistants
is in on this as more words
seep out of the victims' mouths.
"It's when men try to become angels . . ."
No letup on the procession of prisoners.
All in red smocks.
Get the foreshortened view of the dead,
headless, sprawled, wriggling,
each bound to the plank.
Let's have the winds-of-time-
ripping-pages-off-the-calendar shot
superimposed on the racket.
Stick to the facts.
Make seven out of ten victims peasants,
the rest deputies, journalists, big shots,
Girondists, royals, shopkeepers,
over-the-hill Montagnards.
But you'll have to scramble the chronology.
We're working up
to the execution of the Sun King!
—I said don't worry about accuracy—
and the words from the severed heads
have been piling up:
"It's when men try to become angels that they . . ."

Now the Sun King gets his.
—No, hold off on that.
We need more on Big Boy.
The slaughter is incessant.
"Absolute virtue pursued with absolute terror."
The horror draws him in deeper.
Out of the Pol Pot and into the frying pan.
Big Boy on tiptoe.
Unable to predict when a head
will say something, he stares
ever closer into the doomed faces.
Bring on a few notables.
Whenever one of them gets it,
he expects another word—
if not the word incarnate,
then at least a wink.
Let's set up Robespierre.
Put on your panorama hat for this one.
A greater crowd than ever.
Banners: *Liberty Equality Fraternity.*
Flocks of doves. Keep it festive.
Robespierre climbs the scaffold,
or have them lug him up.
Big Boy's lackey wrenches off his coat.
His socks, his stockings fallen,
he's an undignified wreck.
But Big Boy's more than disappointed.
Robespierre, he tried to commit suicide
earlier and only managed to shoot off his jaw.
He can't talk.
Big Boy's more than angry,
he's mean, he's foul, he's vengeful.
He rips the bandages off

and throws them to the creeps on the sidelines,
who fight for them like dogs.
The crowd settles down, stillness.
They know what Big Boy has in mind.
He makes Robespierre wait a long time
before letting the blade drop.

So it goes.
We should have at least one
plaza scene in the rain.
Maybe this one, Charlotte Corday.
She must be beautiful, brunette, gentle.
Too gentle to look like
she could have shoved a dagger
even into the pasty, waterlogged Marat.
Just what was his problem, anyway?
Eczema? V.D.? Skip it.
This is a pivotal scene.
Big Boy searches her eyes
as if she'll tell him the word
while she's still alive.
According to Carlyle, she blushed
when the headsman removed her kerchief.
That's a nice touch. Use it.
Her head falls—slow motion here—
and sure enough, when he lifts her head
—with both hands, pure melodrama,
he's almost reading her lips—
she pronounces an entire word,
three syllables no less,
that sets him back on his heels.
He swoons: three syllables: "resemble."

"It's when men try to become angels
that they most resemble . . ."

Finally, let's skip ahead.
The Sun King, it's curtains for the Sun King
on the shortest day of the year.
And Big Boy's sunk.
The stress has broken him.
He's been taunted, haunted by his victims,
the flesh made word,
but now he's sure that Louie
is good for the terminal word.
But before that the king
has to give a speech.
And I've got just the line.
I forget which, it was either Louis XIV or XVI
who after losing a battle
said, "Has God forgotten
all that I have done for him?"
I don't care who said it, use it.
Have the king, at his own request,
lie face up, staring high into the glare,
so the blade drops, shoots down
as if the sun exploded.
It's always been too heavy a symbol.
The shadow of the blade
hits his throat first.
Slow-motion stop and go.
Big Boy grabs the head by the hair
before it hits the drenched deck
and holds it aloft.
It starts to spin slowly

and he turns with it,
beseeching it, *tête-à-tête*,
his eyes bulging more
than the dead head's.

The people get more excited, believing
Big Boy's displaying it for them.
A tremendous crescendo.
Citizens start to scramble
onto the scaffold, clamoring
to dip their handkerchiefs
in the king's blood.
Big Boy, still awaiting the word,
stamps on their fingers,
tries to stomp them
without taking his eyes off the king.
The crowd bellows and waves,
waves money at him;
those closest to the edge
demand a lock of Louis' hair.
They want to rip his coat apart,
wear strips of it as headbands.
Big Boy refuses, yanks the coat
away from his assistants with one hand.
The crowd begins to jeer him.
Thousands in thunderous unison
take up the disdainful cry,
calling him King Nasty! King Nasty!
. . . King Nasty or King Naughty.
He can't concentrate in the tumult.
He's lost it, he's missed it,
foiled by the bellow and roar

of his own name, his new name.
The king says something—
"It's when men try to become angels
that they most resemble . . ."
but Big Boy loses it
like a drop in the ocean.
This has to happen very fast,
absolutely deafening noise
that ends in absolute silence,
ringing silence
with Big Boy staring deaf and dumb
into god knows what.

That's it for today.
I've given you plenty to go on,
try to kick it into shape.
Put your heads together.
Maybe you can find something else
for that sentence. I'm loose.
Maybe you can come up with a palindrome.
Maybe we got a play here.
Or convert it into an opera.
A musical. Or all three.
We could run a contest.
Instead of that sentence,
the heads can sing a jingle.
Think about casting right away.
Ask the sponsors to suggest somebody.
Anyway, that's it.
Let's have a drink.
How do you like your bourbon?

SELF-PORTRAIT

from Michelangelo Buonarroti's
"I' sto rinchiuso come la midolla"

I live here, a shut-in, poor, alone,
bottled up like a stale genie.
My thoughts can't fly in this dark tomb
without being snared by a thousand cobwebs.
Giants crap outside my door all night
along with countless others
too drunk or too sick to make it home.
The sound of them pissing and puking
wakes me before the morning light.
Cats, carnage, vermin:
my doorstep's a cesspool
no visitor will bother to cross.
My soul has this advantage over my body:
it smells better in there than out here.
It couldn't escape if it wanted to,
one way or the other—My head's clogged
with a cold and I'm constipated.
It must want to leave a body so ruptured,
wrecked, cracked, and split from hard work.
Death's a boarding house
where I live on credit.
My happiness is my dejection,
my rest my discomfort.
When you pray for bad luck,
God should give it.
You who saw me at the Feast of the Magi
know what I mean, know why my house
is a stable among the palaces of the rich.
Love's flame leaves my heart cold.

A great shit would drive out a little care
—this soul of mine
that's had its wings clipped.
My voice sounds like a hornet trapped in a jar.
My gallstones rattle.
My eyes look like blue dust
ground in a black bowl.
My teeth are as loose as a keyboard.
My face is the shape of fear itself.
I'm a wind-shaken scarecrow.
A spider spins a web in one ear
while a cricket chirps all night in the other.
Awake or not, I sound like I'm snoring.
Love, the muse, the flowery grottoes—
all that I've drawn and scribbled
adorns the walls of outhouses, whorehouses, and bars.
What use are all the puppets I've made!
I feel like someone who has swum the ocean
only to drown in the muck offshore.
Art and fame have left me poor and old, not free.
If I don't die first, things will just get worse.

L'INFINITO

Leopardi

This hill has always meant so much to me,
and this hedgerow, near enough to keep
the farthest horizon from my view.
But sitting and watching, I lose myself
in this endless space, wondering what lies beyond,
what peace and quiet, what supreme depth.
So for a while the heart is unafraid.
And when the wind bursts through the trees
I see how far into that infinite silence
this voice can go, and then in an instant
I know what eternity is, the dead seasons,
and the sound of life around me.
So my thought drowns in the middle of it all:
and how sweet to be a castaway in this sea.

from LITTLE TESTAMENT

To awake on my fortieth birthday
buried in this pile of gifts
and not question how they
or I got here
but proceed with the inventory,
all tatters and extra coda,
and salvage for you what I can
from whatever is fake and forgettable:

Something old, something new, something
borrowed, stolen, scavenged,
a lot simply looted
from the pleasures and shambles of the day.

                . . .

Forty years old
and I still can't see myself
planting flowers
on either the dark edge of heaven or hell.

Though in either place
I can guess which would flourish,
I have a better idea
of what thrives here.
Item: And so, instead of a bribe
for my gravekeeper,
I leave a Trillium,

a lovely plant
that smells like rotten meat,
or any other flowering contradiction
whose colors attract bees

but whose stench draws flies;
whose pollination depends
on an insult as well as beauty.

. . .

Item: Now for you, my several friends,
in honor of your trust,
your warmth, your jokes:
Champagne . . . in a dirty glass.
Though not just any glass:
the finest old Venetian,
so light and clear you would think
the Air herself
had placed her hand in yours

and a cool secret on your lips.
How light touches its delicate rim,
curves into serenity with a smirk,
the glint that was in the eye
of its maker, the Venetian
who tried to get glass this thin
believing that it would shatter
if ever a drop of poison
were added to the wine.
It was a doge eat doge world all right.

. . .

Item: And you, occasional poet,
I award you a ton of sympathy,
a place to dump it,
and this variation on a theme:
It's not the heat, it's the humidity.

It's not the squalid kitchen,
the boiled chicken, the burnt sneaker,
the steam in a white sink.

It's not the four million tons
of cosmic dust
that gravity gathers
and drops on earth each day,
it's your own squandered magic,
the weight of your own quiet voice.
It's the peculiar sense of nothing
when the middle of nowhere shifts again.
It's the quiet, disappointing extreme,
another long-deserted drive-in movie
at high noon, titles
still dangling from the marquee
in busted poems, speaker wire
ripped from rusted pipe,
dry weeds in the gravel.
It's the endless intermission,
the stalled ocean,
the blank screen's faded lunar curve
tilted high over the asphalt's faded waves.

. . .

Item: To my wife, Ann,
I leave this littered house
and all it contains:
the comfort, the disarray, the panic,
the splendid lamps
that shine through the oaks,
the windows high and wide,

and the constellation
that we've traced
in winter's long view of the stars.

Each place we've known, each point
a knot in The Great Net,
cast from childhood to Asia, across
the longitude and lassitude of our time;
this notion, that there is
no end to what we are,
that tangled, snagged, and drawn,

the routes of our coming and going
converge here, gathered in the lights
spread over these black hills
and clustered in the city's heights,
for us to haul it in,
full of whatever we've done,
wherever we've been.

Item: To my son, Alexander,
I bequeath with love and admiration
the Arc de Triomphe.
And here's why:
To commemorate
the golden attitude you displayed
in the first moments of your life,
the magnificent arc you made
when the doctor
held you aloft in the cold air
and you twisted and turned,
scattering everyone

in the delivery room
as you pissed all over us.

Item: To my daughter, Helen,
I leave a prime Elysian plot,
that island-meadow
you rode into
late one afternoon
and let your horse wade at will,
stir up wildflower
and milkweed
in the purpling blue,

so that the silver seed
hovered far around you,
made you smile
amid innumerable smiles
and raised in a casual swarm
years of waves and glinting wings.

Whatever favor, whatever truth
there was of Elysium
filled your eyes
and you laughed at the mystery of things
like one of god's spies
when the sun
coaxed your soul into sight
then drew your name
in the air, Loved-of-Light.

Or perhaps you saw it all
in a less mawkish way:

the grinning spirits,
the exaltation of shoppers
as they enter The Celestial Mall.

Item: Dead-eye Dick,
the jubilant realist, where did he go?
And the bouncers
at the Tempus Fugit Funeral Parlor,
who gave them the heave-ho?
Polly and Esther,
the scrawny Ripsnorter
and Capability Jones?
The Fearless Fucker, the Blizzard Dancer,
when the bottles slipped
out of their frozen gloves,
where did they go?
Where does the hasty music lead?
The happy rat tracks in the snow?

What happened to Elmer
and Daffy, Big Bertha and Limp Louie?
Bashful, Happy and Grumpy?
Comatose, Ecstatic and Berserk?
What are all these blanks
in the summer street?
Whatever happened to that guy
who used to catch bullets in his teeth?

To them, to anyone
humbled, stricken by the beauty
the world gives and takes,
here's the long and short of it:

In any of the blooming zeroes
one cloud sprinkles offshore,
in any crater on the moon,
lay down this life.

Item: Now, last readers,
I offer dipsomanic immunity
to any place you wish,
where all you need do
is relax, stroll, hold hands
like absurdity and squalor,
and admire the indolent harbors
and unfinished memorials
to The Spirit of Laziness.

Where bridges and hours span a mile or two more
than they did before,
confident splendors
suspended above the monstrous clamor,
the furious view
of another life below.

Where you don't have to spend
nights in a damp park
listening to swans fart in their sleep.
No more mornings that leave you
dizzy and stranded
on a pile of junk and generosity
or meandering
through zoos in rainlight,
the steamy cages,
the great apes whimpering in the mists,

the washed-out posters
announcing yet another concert
by Smug Paul and the Hedonists.
Now, for you, the tidal music
of evening resumes,
with its dockside antics and lunar revelry,
the private balcony
from which you can watch divers
as their flashlights
scan the harbor floor
for the pianos you've tossed to them.

Here's the chance
to catch up on sleep you lost long ago.
Find a loose hour or two
in a pile of rose leaves
steeped in sunlight and spilled wine,
in the kindlier motions
of silence and vagrant time,

that may wake you on the move,
like the only birds in an early breeze,
like fish in a strong current,
like dirty spirits in starlight
—wake on the silver heels
of gods who vanish into their own jokes.

Item: Until then, forget all this clutter
but take this pearl.
It is the hard light, the soul
of the laziest thing that ever lived.
I didn't get around to—

I couldn't decide what to wrap it in,
which unfinished poem
or squandered conceit.

It would be easier
just to rip a page out of a book,
one that I remember describes
how in World War II
the writer Malaparte
while crossing the Lake Lagoda convoy route
during the siege of Leningrad
looked down through the ice at one point
and saw innumerable human faces,
beautiful glass masks,
staring up at him.

Their lips thin and worn,
their hair long, their eyes large and clear
like delicate icons—the images of those
killed while attempting to cross
the only supply line to a ruined city.

Their bodies, submerged all winter,
had been swept away
by the first spring currents,
but the expression their faces
had left etched in the ice,
he said it was serene
and that their eyes seemed to follow his
as he walked across the lake.

Or instead of that page,
I could use those stanzas by Arnaut Daniel
that Pound translated:

"Though all things freeze here,
    I can naught feel the cold,
For new love sees, here
    my heart's new leaf unfold;
So am I rolled
    and lapped against the breeze here:
Love, who doth mould
    my force, force guarantees here.

"Aye, life's a high thing,
    where joy's his maintenance,
Who cries 'tis a wry thing
    hath danced never my dance,
I can advance
    no blame against fate's tithing
For lot and chance
    have deemed the best thing my thing."

Or, instead of wrapping the pearl,
why don't I just roll it over to you,
ahead of the morning.
Let your eyes grow accustomed to it
as they did to the depths of the night,
and find how between your fingertips
it is a toy of thought.
Seed of obstinance, prize
of mood, sand and tide,
it is not the ball of light

that others wish the world to be
but what little sense
it can yield in a year and a day.
It is my own gift of darkness,
less than I mean, all I can say.

The Curious Builder

WET BREAD AND ROASTED PEARLS

Through a filmstrip of train windows,
I watch the river coast by, mist
climb the Palisades to open sky.

Hudson Line. Gravel trackbed
dusted with snow, bank rock and piling
blackened with oil, barges
half-rotted on granite slabs
where a deer dips her head in bent reeds

and then steps out onto shore ice:
One long wave of white ice
nightwinds caught at its farthest reach
between arrival and return
and held gleaming above the tide.

The ideogram for "recognition,"
you know, was formed from the figure
of a deer: to leap from a standstill.
And when the thin ice
suddenly collapses
and I see the doe slide, stagger,

but somehow remain on a wobbling piece
that carries her
out into the mist—there's
the ideogram for "amazement":
to be standing in that splendor.

Blue cliffs lean against bluer sky,
blue as the wreaths
around smokers' heads,

sleepers' heads, readers' heads;
blue as the blurred tattoo on his arm,
the old man in the next seat:
the tall ship faded into his skin.

Once across the city line
riverbank turns to rubble.
Row after row of mounds,
a ransacked graveyard
of mistakes buried under broken images,
brick, busted block, scrap metal,
crumpled sheetrock, tires,
charred planks, sand piles
dumped on lots
glittering with crushed glass.

Of the numerous ideograms
for "to fill in the blanks"
one is based on a recognizable figure
heaving gigantic hourglasses
off a train just before it bursts
under a roaring city
and stalls.

Another contains
a figure, someone who abhors
crossword puzzles, someone
like me, newspaper
in hand, stultified
by a maze of blanks.

Eighty-nine down: More lavish clues.

One across: To be reasonably
suspicious of zeros and words
that contain too many o's.

Two across: Prosopopoeia.

Fifty-five down: Monotonous.

Three across: Puzzle is to Mystery
as Grapefruit is to. . .

Five across: Rhymes with orange.

Eight across: Of Aquitaine, as in:

Thirteen across: Of summertime, as in:

I think I'll throw away a poem, take
a nap and then go stand in the sun.
Or lie beside you on the dock awhile
and write another one.

Or wait for you to open your eyes
and figure out
what this little kid on the beach
is all about.

He's pulverized pearls with a rock
after he popped them
like corn in a fire,
a handful of fake pearls
he cast on the water

along with some bread for
Thirty-four down: Type of fish,
a.k.a. "pumpkin seeds."

Crumbs and pearl dust—sunnies
rise out of the murk
like stupidity approaching speech,
then veer off
without a nibble, without a blink.

And, like Twenty-one across:
A magician
who somehow tricks himself,
makes his own charms
disappear and finds himself
empty-handed in the unyielding air,
the kid just stands there
staring at a puddle of oil
that floats between dock and raft,
its slack colors slipping away
like The Lost Planet, turning
with every move this one ever made.
And whatever made it move:

Gases change to moiling seas,
squashed continent to coastline.
Greenery fades to saltflat
and back again.
Empire and ignorance,
each with its course, its color
—a different color for every age,
every eon, migration and flood,

dust and flood, famine
and soaked plunder, flight
and pursuit, white and yellow
and blue, the aerial swirl of snow
and disease, peace
and convulsion, belief and denial.
And there it goes, sight out of mind,
leaving me

to watch you finally wake
and wonder what dreamt you into being;
to almost know it, but to lose
that, too, in shadow and water,
and then watch reappear
another circling fly, another
horsefly and gnat, dragonflies
and, Twenty-one down:

the "wizardry in daylight"
that allows them to stay,
suspended
in the ever-expanding sky
that sweeps back
to Thirteen down: Bombay,
where one afternoon, leaving
that city on a slow, quiet train,
trackbed raised
above flooded fields,
no land in sight,
I could see nothing
but sky mirrored in water
and the tremendous sun drawing

its hour-long reflection
across horizonless blue.

Two perfect circles, swirling,
identical,
slid into one, hung there,
where an early world
that greeted the advent of yellow
with flutes and bells
and pure geometry,
intersects Thirty-four across:

The Grapefruit,
the one you thought I'd aimed at you
just because it punctured the wall
next to your ear.
The glaring, almost magical fact of it,
a grapefruit stuck in sheetrock.

One warm afternoon, hillside
yellow with fallen leaves, starlings
began to flock, as plentiful
as the leaves still left in the maples.
All that clatter, so many,
thrown every which way
in the shrapnel wind,
people stepped warily out their door
and wondered what was going on.

Even we, who had seen it before,
could only raise our arms
and laugh at what was as much

a feeling as a sight,
a sound, the sky-blown praise,
the mayhem, the soft yellow ground

now as blank as Eight down,
the winter you decided
to freeze me out, kept
the house as cold as a morgue.

Days I didn't hear
you speak except in your sleep,
so that one morning I woke
to the sound of your voice
and a cold draft

and the noisy sparrows
at the window.
I lay there cold and tired
listening to Five down: The first sign
of spring, cheap-talk
in the dismal, breaking light.

And when the smoke alarm,
its battery worn down,
began to beep, the signal
at first indistinguishable
from the birdcalls
but then growing louder,
triumphantly monotonous
in their absence, I remained
Three down:
A man of my word.

And that word is
Fifty-five across: Disingenuous.

For the rest of that week
above Peekskill Hollow Road
the ridge loomed, fledged with treetops
rising row behind row.
By the next, the colors
had flown, and for days
in that gray intricacy
of italics and twigs,
the slightest sound reached
a distant, whispered edge: pencil

scraping paper, dry leaves
blown over pavement; a vine
rubbing stone; a piece
of cellophane flying out of nowhere
on that remote lake, skidding
after me as I skated.
And suddenly, as if I were
the figure on the cover
of Two down: a novel
of grim pursuit, regret
and Gothic dread,

there was, inexplicably,
more cellophane,
scraps of clarity, a swarm
of blanks and withered smiles
whirling around me
before I simply turned

and headed back into the wind,
scraping a few more edge songs
out of what stays, what goes. . .

what happens when we
find ourselves in Eighty-nine across:
An Important Event
in the History of Punctuation:

We lie in the dark and listen.
The window open
you wait for me to guess
what you already know:
that voice so lovely and strange
you can't believe
I don't remember what it is.
And then I do:

Miles of lake ice shift and thaw,
singing the changes
that move as lightly as years
and the lifelong questioning
that keeps turning me toward you
and One down: The origin
of the question mark

in darkness and the curve and line
of your spine, your neck,
your chin, your ears, your
legs and breasts and my open hands
—Hands, rough, calloused,
sliding over your taut silk
they sound like breath.

SUBMISSION

Dear Editor,

After three years of receiving impersonal rejection slips
from you, this is my last shot—though, I think, my best. I'd
like to see you do better (see attached). Aren't editors sup-
posed to encourage talent? I'd like to see what you'd come up
with if you worked behind a counter watching people eat
eggs all day, or if 30% of your clientele drove up with Head-
of-Jesus decals on their highbeams!

But I am not an unreasonable man, nor an imperceptive
one. I can detect an editor's preference and respond with-
out necessarily diluting my own aesthetic standards. I just
think an occasional forthrightness on your part would spare
your more daring readers a lot of uncertainty. If it's alleolin-
ear autorimic quasi-spondaic pyrrhic monometer you want,
why not flat out say so?

> Hells bells
> to you,
>
> Peewee

Enc: Prime-Time Claptrap

PRIME-TIME CLAPTRAP

Willy-nilly,
Sweetmeat
murdered
slopshop
fat cat,
forswore
voodoo,
kidded
dreaded
downtown
bigwig,
feted
rich-bitch
redhead,
bedded
dreamteam
polo
hotshot,
headed
bozo's
May Day
wingding,
shredded
London-
Hong Kong
airfare,
wedded
wide-eyed
true blue
roly-poly
nitwit.
Teehee.

Boohoo.

POLICE BLOTTER

4:31 A.M.	Call for assistance. Brawl at Harmony Diner. Blotter entry only.
4:38	Numerous complaints of foul-mouthed crowd at Fair Haven Cottages. Complainants advised and consoled.
6:00	Jehovah's Witnesses advise they will visit certain neighborhoods in the morning.
8:20	Rambunctious peddle-twats loitering near laundromat.
9:10	Wanwood Road resident reports prowler licking her window. Assign: 434/Towle.
	434 verifies tongue print on plate glass. Largest he has ever seen. Requests backup.
9:45	Hostile dogs on Bontemps Road.
9:47	Campers request medical assistance for bee stings. Five hikers stung on tongue have fled into woods.
10:08	Complaints of lugubrious violins on Bluebird Drive. Assign 444/North.
10:10	Reports from Cedar Ledges area. Jehovah's Witnesses pestering residents.

10:23   Librarian requests assistance. Dictionaries
         appear to have exploded during the night.
         Assign: 482/Fagin.

         482 reports verbal shrapnel, ustulated walls
         and ceiling, anile staff inexplicably jubilant.

11:00   Wildwood resident calls third time this week
         to report vine strangling tree in front yard.

11:00   Report from Cedar Ledges: naked nullifidian
         hosing down proselytizers.

11:00   Wildwood resident insists that "a vine,
         like love, kills what it clings to."

11:22   Aggressive harmonica playing at Star Gardens.
         Assign: 444/North.

         444 returning with 5 suspects shackled & gagged.

1:06   Power lines down at Memorial Stadium, dam break
P.M.   on Memory Lane, fissures in earth's crust.
         Blotter entry only.

1:18   Principal requests armed assistance
         at elementary school. Children's kites
         assaulted and ravaged by hawks.
         Assign: 461/Hershon.

         461 reports subject offers extensive
         possibilities for haiku.

2:47 Long Meadow resident reports diminutive woodland creatures pouring pearls over feet of unidentified nude in sunlit clearing. Assign: 482/Fagin.

5:16 461 has distraught woman in custody. Subject admits she has debilitating sense of irony. Having read that Nero's teacher was a Stoic caused relapse. Subject detained, pacified, insulted and released.

7:00 Night manager complains of vociferous, moose-ugly youths congregating in front of Bubba's Market. Assign: 444/North.

444 reports youths have turned darkly sarcastic, requests backup. All units.

9:42 Anonymous caller wants to know if world was created *ex nihilo* or if God created it out of part of himself; if latter possibility most likely, which part might God have used? All units confer.

9:43 Caller advised to look around and consider which part of himself he would donate to such an end. Caller rejects advice as "puerile anthropomorphism," refuses to identify himself, laughs and hangs up.

10:28 Attempts to trace call abandoned.

10:30   Sunnydale resident reports winged children
        playing with fire.
        Referred to Fire Department.

11:14   Medical assistance requested at Harmony Diner
        for subject suffering allergic reaction to
        symmetry. Assign 434, 482/Towle and Fagin.

11:25   Officers confirm subject covered with hives
        after viewing new Palladian tile floor
        and that the hives have broken out
        in a symmetrical pattern.

11:28   Call from Shady Hollow Arts Colony. Routine
        neo-Platonic squabble over whether beauty is
        better apprehended through sight or sound
        has escalated into armed combat.
        Musicians in full retreat.
        Alert all units.

        Units refuse to respond, cite general lack
        of interest. Compare outcome to watching
        a snail swallow a slug. Advise both sides
        be given ample time to bury their dead.

11:59   Village Square residents report gigantic
        flying brains have entered park.
        Attack imminent.
        Assign: 461/Hershon.

        461 on location, reports size of brains
        exaggerated, minor property damage,
        situation resolved.

SCATTER

Thank you for writing and we are happy
to respond to your inquiries.

Yes, it was Pericles who used the masts
of captured warships to build the Odeum;
Hugh Capet's son was Robert the Debonair,
and the Inca road system was comparable
to Rome's, but Romans had more words
for sex than Eskimos have for ice formations.
The air brake was invented in 1869,
the Rhetorical Wrench in 1844,
and "prurient" is the most quiet word
in the language, which is English,
and which, you'll be pleased to know,
happens to describe the afterlife
more relentlessly than most.
This should also be of interest to you
since, indeed, there is life after death,
even though it is extremely brief,
only a moment really; but keep in mind
that the closer you get to the sun
the slower time revolves, so
in that one sweeping moment
you may well get the chance
to tell your heart's desire
that she was made for the light
and to hold each other as knowingly
as roses and grapevines
climbing the same sun-shot trellis.
Then, again, you may find yourself
giving a speech that enthralls
your audience but, because you have
no idea what the subject is, keeps you
clinging to the incomprehensible

like a fly to glass, until they
abruptly, inexplicably, shift
their attention with no loss
of intensity to the sight
of chimney smoke mingling with steam
from a nearby clothes dryer vent,
or to a mutilated toad
the cat proudly presented,
or to drivers slowing down as you
did one spring afternoon
to watch two ancient sisters
emerge from their swayback house
to trim great, blooming, sail-high lilacs
in the same long-awaited wind that turns
the contrails of vanished planes
into night clouds thinner than the chalk
smears your swirling eraser wiped off
the blackboard behind you where beside
The Seven Lamps of Architecture,
The Seven Champions of Christendom,
Seven Pillars of Wisdom, Seven
Deadly Sins, Seven Liberal Arts,
Seven Sleepers of Ephesus, Seven
Sages of Rome, Seven Types
of Ambiguity, The Seven Wonders
of the Ancient and Modern Worlds,
The Seven Sacraments, The Seven
Cities of Gold and The Seven Dwarfs,
you should have written The Seven
Sisters, The Seven Continents,
Seven Against Thebes, Seven Brides
for Seven Brothers, The Seven Samurai,
The Magnificent Seven and 7-Up.

MORE ON THE HEROIC DEEDS AND MANNER OF THE WORTHY RABELAIS, DOCTOR OF MEDICINE

"Rabelais," Pantagruel continued, "was a marvelous person
to see and know even when he was hung-over.

"If he smiled, it was roses, junkyard roses;

"If he sneered, it was an ox waking up in a honey pit;

"If he sighed, it was bygones;

"If he blinked, you could hear it.

"If he was angry, it was How to Embarrass an Idealist;

"If he was pleased, it was hammers, it was sparks flying off nailheads at twilight;

"If he was in a good mood, you knew it was the storm's paraph;

"If he spat, he spat moths.

"If he was queasy, it was Closed for Alterations printed on his eyelids;

"If he was worried, the sky was an erased Tiepolo;

"If he was complimentary, it was palm readers slapped across the face;

"If he had a sneezing fit, it was roadside yo-yo, it was the same cloud of flies blown off a dead raccoon again and again by speeding Chrysler Imperials.

"If he slept well, it was Aristotle, Aristotle, Aristotle;

"If he didn't, it was plumbic odes for breakfast;

"If he didn't sleep at all, it was Kierkegaard and beans.

"If he scribbled, it was a pile of rope;

"If he sketched, it was Pleasure Seekers at 2 A.M.;

"If he painted, ripples it was on the surface but Milton and Beethoven, deaf and blind and furious three fathoms below, groping, jabbing and screaming at each other eternally.

"If he murmured, it was soil enriched with dragon blood;

"If he vomited, it was historical, it was Hannibal pouring boiling vinegar on Alpine slopes so his troops wouldn't slip on the ice;

"If he just belched, it was fiction and any resemblance to actual persons or places purely coincidental and gladly welcome.

"If he was love-struck, it was Leda and the Swan, it was the Boss Swan Overture, it was wings gulping white and gold, it was fly her into a standstill, it was crucial creatures stirring up realms of trouble;

"If mere lust, it was Leda and the Duck, your common poker flip-flipping along the muck-edge of things.

"If he was perplexed, it was a crow and its shadow goose-stepping over a snowbank;

"If attentive, it was an upright groundhog;

"If he twitched and drooled, it was the Alemanni stammering into a lambent temple;

"If he went drinking again, he'd invite his favorite fallacies:

"If it was *ad hominem*, it was Have one on me and grow real tired of yourself long before you die;

"If *ad misericordium*, Could you spare a glass of water?

"If *petitio principii*, Tequila with an empty bucket on the side, please;

"If *non sequitur*, a shot of whiskey with a coffee chaser;

"If *ad baculum*, it was Let's dribble the bouncer.

"If he had too much Barolo, it was Hey, look at these flesh-colored tattoos;

"If it was Chardonnay, it was a cool draft from a mine shaft, cool as a flute;

"If it was Chianti, it was twelve gauge, it was a bat hunt in formal attire;

"If it was strong ale, The gods love an intelligent slut;

"If weak ale, it was starving prisoners waiting for their fingernails and hair to grow into a snack;

"If it was rum and tea, it was Merry Morning Melodies;

"If it was champagne and brandy, it was 'cheerful stoicism,' it was pensioned gladiators, it was gladiolas, glad to be here, glad to be of help, glad to see you, glad to see you go.

"And the strange thing was that even if it was well water, he never knew when to shut up."

ERRATA

muttering about a tumultuous void,/he
retired from the railroad."

5   After "disappointed," place inverted
      exclamation point.

50   26   After "a loner amongst the natives," add "stood
          motionless for 19 hours 25 seconds/on July 20
          at the Motionless Festival in Indonesia."

     30   After "broken English," place inverted
          question mark.

     31   Omit "difficult," add "money-hungry, bug-eyed,
          sex-starved, hog-wild."

72   9   After "became patron saint of thieves,"
          add "Hermes."

     10   After "The ancients sucked in the last breath
          of their expiring friends," add "maybe."

     15   Omit "Rest In Peace," omit "Get Lost!" Omit
          "He Never Had A Clue." Add "plagiarized
          epitaph," add "I will miss myself."

Fracas

THE ANAMORPHOSIS

I

Now you are looking into the eyes of a man who woke up with an ear the size of a tuba. There's no telling how it happened. Fact is, he woke up that way, the strange effect of a lost cause. He thought he was dreaming at first, riding high dark seas on a half-deflated life raft. But no, he lay sprawled on his own bed, clinging to his own ear, his tremendous ear.

With a pinch or two, a short slide along a decidedly auricular swirl, his fingertips confirmed it: the *most* remote, bloodless part of him, a lump of involuted insensitivity, had become the most—the ... most ... the most of him. He lay there listening to the sun rise, the darkness dwindle, the gentlest thing he'd ever heard. Water trickled, pipes trembled, the reheated house began to creak and stretch as if rising in his stead, high above him, while his great sponge of an ear continued to soak up his own being. Egads. Whatever could it mean? Another day, another undeserved problem. To one who has lived alone too long, life is especially treacherous.

What propels that whirling stillness in his eyes? Panic? That's one way of looking at it. A kind of sadness? Yes. Grief? Abandonment? Possibly. Medieval diagnoses tumble forth: his deformity is punitive, a pleasure-hound's comeuppance, Pinocchio's countercharge, the result of being morally depraved or spiritually deprived. Or perhaps it's the effect of an overly solemn political view of art or an irredeemably comic awareness of his own condition. We can only wonder. At this moment, he simply recalls that the guardian of dreams had a brother, Momus, the god of ridicule. And, of course, that he's going to be late for work—again.

What else can rouse him to defy his fate? He does all he can do: he listens. He drools a little and listens. Car ignitions, the raggedy firing of untuned engines, the hum and flow of distant traffic, quickened footsteps from blocks away, stalwart citizens heading off to meaningful employment, the skirl of factory-whistle pipes: what he hears begins to sound heaven-sent, the music of prosperity, the promise of life-defining work calling to him—work and what begins to feel like salvation.

Can he sit up? No, but, by god, he tries. He twists himself half off the bed, kneeling, dragging his head along the mattress, and hoists himself up the bedpost. He tries to stand free, but unable to straighten his neck—so lopsided is he, his earlobe alone weighs more than a wet sandbag, a sack of chicken feed slung over his shoulder—he begins to totter and sway like a drunk on a tightrope. He crashes hard, the enormous plunger of an ear squashed, stuck to the cold floor. All he can do is stay there, sucking up a colder silence until all he can hear is his own heartbeat trapped—kathump-kathump-kathump— bouncing like wearied sonar off the earth's vast and empty core.

The blank of fatalism has refilled his eyes. But not for long. His ear has indeed shrunk a bit. Gradually, the suction relents and pops him to freedom. He embraces his ear and his fate and squeezes the weight out of both of them. As he compresses his ear, he can feel his determination swell like grandeur. He squirms across the floor and shoves himself through the door to daylight, to his job, his life's work, drawn by a music more powerful than gravity. . .

II

It's the Science and Nature Section
and we're leaving.
No, it's the Sociology Section.
No matter, make a right.
Don't shove, don't push,
keep your place in line,
don't litter,
don't act silly,
and we'll be out of here
in a minute.

Don't throw anything.
Don't climb on anything.
And don't interrupt—I said
don't interrupt.

Stay in line.
How should I know what
a Bride of Quietness is?
Raise your hand.
No, that's a fruit bat.
No, I can't explain
the lascivious grin.
Yes, they're all depraved.
Next time, raise your hand.

No, we're not in the basement.
It's the Social Science Gallery.
Stop bouncing that ball.
Nobody buffs an armadillo.
They're born that way—smudge-free.

Don't touch.
Keep moving.
Yes, it looks like an attic.
Make a right.
No, we're not lost.
O.K. it is the basement.
Tie your shoelace.
Next corridor turn right.

Put that back.
This is not the attic.
I don't know the longest
one-syllable word in the language.

Keep going straight.
Yes, that is the longest
one-syllable word in the language.
Thank you!

We're not lost, we're back
in the Science and Nature Section.
Don't touch.
It's a portrait.
I don't know what it's doing here.
It's Stalin.
It says: "The muzhik
looked into his eyes and saw
the well where the devil drowned."
You don't know what a muzhik is?
Tough.

That's called a diorama.
How should I know?
Some kind of thatched
and tropical hebetude.
Does that help?
Too bad.
Don't touch.
Drop the bongo.

Keep up.
No stragglers.
Stay in line.
We're heading out.
Bejugglements coming up.
It's my word against yours,
and mine is bejugglement.

Stop singing, stop humming,
stop the yammering.
You want to boost a groundling?
You want heckfire and brimstone?
Blood and coal?
Theological, biological
and literary knickknacks?
You want feathered serpents
and spiky demons?
Then stop yammering.

No, read the caption:
It's an Etruscan hubcap.

That's a finch, the perky finch.
Yes, indeed, the seagull
is a songbird.

That's parchment, a bestiary.
You're supposed to guess:
"Born to bury himself all life long,
swelling the earth with his silence,
always seeking a darker blindness,
a deeper grave, the fearful—"
Give up?
It's Elmo the Mole!

Stop sniveling.
Keep moving.
We're not lost.
This might be the Art & Leisure Annex,
or it might be
the Social Science Gallery.
Who knows?
No, you can't take a nap.

I don't know what that means.
Try this one.
It's a prow, it's a Viking longboat,
it's killer elegance.
It's Svend, fork-bearded Svend
gazing fiercely into *Mare Tenebrosum*.
Does that help?

Then try this one.
It's a piece of something
by Bernard Palissy.
It says, "16th Century Ceramicist.
Burned down his own house
to keep his furnace going
just to finish it—whatever it was."

Let's keep moving.
No, it doesn't mean
whatever you want it to mean.
It's a flaming skeleton
racing across a field of daisies
and it means "Death of a Solipsist."

That's called
The Pleasure-hound's Lament.
The caption's in Latin.
It says, "My heart is a cliché
jammed inside a stale fortune cookie."

We're not lost.
No napping, keep moving.
That's right,
it's called *Love's Arrows
Deflected by Chastity's Shield.*

No, you can't take a nap.
Look at this one.
What do you see?

Another profoundly bamboozled visage?
You think so?

But step to the right,
way over, and look at it sideways.
Now what do you see?
A man with an ear the size of what?
A tuba? A coffee table?
Pretty interesting, huh?
Wake up! I said no napping.

Look, you know what a tableau is?
You know what sequins are?
You know what "bathos" means?
Well, after you've figured
this one out,
make a right, keep going
until you come to the sequined bathos
of Sweet Petunia
and Her Twinkling Hefties Quintet.
I'll be waiting for you.
Wake me up when you get there.

BATHOS

One or two, it seems, turn up
each spring, not far off a road
where they'd wandered into the woods
until they dropped in the snow and froze,
providing filler for the local paper:
another middle-aged male,
unidentified, decomposed.

Reading about one of them yet again,
the usual list of what he wore,
how many shirts, pants, jackets,
socks, I find myself sliding back
into the same sad and hollow poem
I've tried to write before,
about how a person,
an all-American misfit,
moving from place
to place, job to job, can keep
putting on one self after another
without sloughing any off,
growing heavier but more hollow
with each menial part he has to play.

And so it goes, a half-formed poem
spun out of images of luck and loss,
rag and bone, soul and husk.
And when I think I'm at the point
where I can wrap it up in silences
that peel away, onion-like, or open
like a weak hand or, finally,
a mummy, empty, unraveling
as it's slowly twirled,

afloat amid dim stars and its own dust,
the poem stalls. I'm sidetracked again,
remembering myself, like so many others
who wandered around for a while
when young, in Afghanistan, in Nepal,
Turkey, Bulgaria, Spain,
getting dressed before going to sleep,
putting on all I had to ward off the cold.
I see myself again, in Amsterdam,
an impetuous kid on a Sunday morning,
April 9th, nineteen sixty-eight,
with a ticket home, a flight to catch,
but no money to pay the hotel bill.
How I got dressed again and again,
reluctant to leave anything behind, pulling
khaki pants over dungarees, tucking
flannel shirts under cotton shirts,
shoving a manuscript, a couple of years
of turgid poems, under my belt and,
finally, shoving myself into a blue suit
that'd been stuffed into a knapsack
for a couple of years. Sweating, barely
able to bend my knees or arms,
I lurch through the lobby, telling
the suspicious manager I'm off to church.

I try to hitchhike to the airport
but all I get are wary looks.
I still arrive early. Too early:
The check-in counter is closed.
Days without a meal, I want to be
first on line, first on the plane,

first seat from the galley.
Tired, woozy, I every so often
lean back to read the clock overhead.
I'm asleep on my feet, unaware
of the crowd forming behind me.
Again I open my eyes, lean back,
look up, but stumble, and as I feel
my shoe heel roll over something,
crush something soft but solid,
I hear a groan of agony
so profound my stomach knots up.
I turn in time to catch him as he falls.
His eyes squeezed tight, he tries to speak.
His eyebrows are slightly tweezed.
Tears run down his cheeks; his cheeks
are lightly powdered and rouged.
His hair, a shade darker than natural,
is finely cut and he's wearing
a long mink coat that matches his hair.
Trembling, crumbling, he leans on the man
next to him, also draped in mink
the same color as his dyed hair.
His face is powdered, too—It's Liberace?
Yes, it's Liberace and his friend!
I look down, we're all looking down
at his friend's foot, the shoeless one,
covered by a thick white sock.

Doubled over, he's trying to speak.
I try to pick up his cane
with my free hand, but packed
into my suit, poetry manuscript stiff

as a board against my stomach,
I can't stretch, can't reach it.
I'm afraid he's going to pass out.
Unbelievably, he attempts a joke:

"Of all the gasp feet of all the toes gasp behind you gasp you had to gasp step on the broken one! Unnnggnnhhgggh!" He slumps, collapses. A call for tickets makes the crowd close in. I try to help, try to hold him upright while sputtering apologies. But Liberace, looking at me, the way I'm moving, lurching backwards now, arms outstretched, clearing the way as we move along the corridor, my wrinkled suit about to burst, tells me, very politely, very firmly, but with something like dread rising in his voice, "Forget it, please. It's nothing, nothing at all. I insist, really. I'm telling you: Will you *please* stay the hell away from us!"

ON AN ACURA INTEGRA

Please think of this as not merely a piece
Of writing that anyone would fully
Appreciate, but as plain and simple
Words that attempt to arouse whatever
Appetencies you, especially, depend
Upon language to fulfill; that drench you
In several levels of meaning at once,
Rendering my presence superfluous.
In other words, welcome this as a poem,
Not merely a missive I've slowly composed
And tucked under your windshield wiper
So that these onlookers who saw me bash
In your fender will think I'm jotting down
The usual information and go away.

MAYHEM WITH DIMWIT

As soon as the patio was finished
they invited their parents
and cousins up for the weekend.
His father had a bad heart, very bad,
and he made weak jokes
   I'll take it any way I can get it!
whenever they warned him to take it easy.
   Stop trimming those shrubs!
They thought he was joking at dinner
when he quietly laid his face
on the picnic table, but when he turned
blue and fell off the bench
they screamed and jumped, calling
neighbors to call the police.
They took turns giving him CPR,
took turns shouting advice
at whoever was giving it.
   Press harder! Pinch his nose!
In the middle of all this
   Didja get the ambulance?
the man who lives in the summer house
next door ambled down the road,
as he does the first day
he arrives every June,
to talk with each neighbor, one
at a time, in his loud,
onerously formal way.
Now he leaned over the hedge,
peered deeply into the mayhem and
   Hello there! What's new?
   How's every little thing?
At one point, the stricken man's

daughter-in-law, on her knees
beside him, looked up and around,
wondering if she could have
actually heard someone ask
   You folks just up for the day?
before a shudder of denial
ran up her spine and she was
swept back into the panic
   My God! Where's the ambulance?
   Will ya try again, for Chrissake?
   Nice job you did on the patio.
   Do you hear any sirens yet?
   He's gone!
   I hope it stays like this all summer.
   No! Press harder!
   Did you buy that slate in Peekskill?

ONE SUMMER AFTERNOON IN THE BACK BAY

It was that second-floor apartment,
corner of Commonwealth & Mass. Ave.
The cops burst in, guns drawn.
They leapt through the doorways,
landing with legs spread, gun barrels
and eyes synchronized, scanning the rooms.
But it was the wrong place, a bum steer.
Even so, Fortin and whatever-his-name-was
refused to stop or acknowledge them.
The game was too close to call.
They had shoved the furniture aside,
taken the pictures off the wall
—converted the living room
into a handball court.
In shorts, sneakers, headbands,
sweating like mad, they played
with a jaw-clenching intensity
that drew the cops over.
One looked at me, jutted his chin,
jerked his thumb toward the game.
I answered with a shrug, showed him
my hands, palms up, explanationless.
They holstered their pistols and watched
as serves were met with a dive, a leap,
a floor-slamming lunge that made
the tone arm bounce across "Rainy Day Women."
It was ferocious, electrifying:
Swipe, snatch, skid, slap, whizzing arms
and volleys, flying sweat, muttered curses.
The cops were as captivated as I was,
the first time any of us had seen
the game played without a ball.

No-ball Handball: and yet not one point,
not one out-of-bounds call was disputed.
And when Fortin finally put
the game away, punched in a shot
that left what's-his-name
looking dumb and deflated,
he walked over dripping, breathless,
gave the invisible ball
one more sharp bounce off the floor,
and to welcome any post-game
commentary greeted the cops
with a triumphantly aw-shucks,
all-American-sportsman smile.
But the cops were already
backing out into the hallway,
the last one with his hands held chest high,
a wary pushing-off motion, a way
of saying, Let's just . . . Just . . . Let's
just . . . just . . . Just let's . . .

QUICK SKETCH

Five years old, she inspects her new home.
She wants a yellow room, new friends.

She walks down the road,
wearing a bikini, high rubber boots
and a black lace shawl,
and introduces herself to the neighbors.

She asks me again, "What happened
to the dark stars?"
          I still don't know.

She says she has no idea
who trimmed the cat's whiskers.
She knows I don't believe her.

She says, "It's unfortunate
that god is invisible."
          I disagree.

She offers me another
butter-and-watermelon sandwich.

I say, "Sure. Pass the mustard."

HUGGERMUGGER

Ctesias:

The last enemies against whom Cyrus fought
were Scythians from Margiana, hoity-toity,
who were led by King Amoreaus, hot-shot.
These people, mounted on elephants, holy moly,
ambushed the Persians, helter-skelter,
and put them to rout, higgledy-piggledy.
Cyrus himself fell from his horse, humpty-dumpty,
and a lance pierced his thigh: low-blow booboo.
Three days later, he died from the wound, loco.

Herodotus:

After decades of warfare, Cyrus, wheeler-dealer,
perished in combat against the armies, super-duper
of Queen Thomyris, hoochie-coochie,
who had long desired to avenge, rough stuff,
the death of her son, namby-pamby.
She ordered the body of Cyrus dragged, ragtag,
from beneath the slain and his head, harum-scarum,
thrown into a vat of blood. Jeepers creepers.
She then commanded the lifeless conqueror: "Drink
this blood, after which you ever thirsted, but
by which your thirst was never allayed, jelly belly!"

Xenophon:

Cyrus died tranquilly in his bed, fancy schmancy.
He had been forewarned in a dream, hocus pocus,
by a man with such a majestic bearing that he

appeared much more than mortal: razzle-dazzle.
"Prepare yourself," he told Cyrus, "for you will
soon be in the company of the gods, hobnob."
Cyrus awoke and offered sacrifices, solo,
on a nearby mountaintop, sky-high,
not to implore the gods, hanky-panky,
to prolong his life, but to thank them, lovey dovey,
for their protection. Three days later, payday,
he gently breathed his last. Okey-dokey.

Lucian:

Cyrus died of grief. Itsy-bitsy.
He was over one hundred years old, fuddy-duddy,
and he was inconsolable because his son, crumbum,
had killed most of his friends, brain drain.
But his son paid him all honors after his death,
building a tomb for him at Passagarda, grandstand,
a city Cyrus had built on the very spot, hot-spot,
where he had vanquished Astyages, who was none other
than his own grandfather. Wowie-zowie. Even-steven.

EXTENUATING CIRCUMSTANCES

I don't know how fast I was going
but, even so, that's still
an intriguing question, officer,
and deserves a thoughtful response.
With the radio unfurling
Beethoven's Ode to Joy, you might
consider anything under 80 sacrilege.
Particularly on a parkway as lovely
as the one you're fortunate enough
to patrol—and patrol so diligently.
A loveliness that, if observed
at an appropriate rate of speed,
affords the kind of pleasure
which is in itself a reminder
of how civilization depends
on an assurance of order and measure,
and the devotion of someone
like yourself to help maintain it.
Yes, man the measurer!
The incorrigible measurer.
And admirably precise measurements
they are—not, of course, as an end
in themselves but, lest we
forget, as a means to propel
us into the immeasurable,
where it would be anybody's guess how fast
the West Wind was blowing
when it strummed a rainbow
and gave birth to Eros.
Never forget that a parkway
is a work of art, and the faster
one goes, the greater the tribute

to its power of inspiration,
a lyrical propulsion that approaches
the spiritual and tempts—demands—
the more intrepid of us
to take it from there.
That sense of the illimitable,
when we feel we are more the glory
than the jest or riddle of the world
—that's what kicked in, albeit
briefly, as I approached
the Croton Reservoir Bridge.
And on a night like this, starlight
reignited above a snowfall's last
flurry, cockeyed headlights scanning
the girders overhead, eggshell
snowcrust flying off the hood,
hatching me on the wing
like a song breaking through prose,
the kind I usually sing
through my nose:

> *So much to love,*
>   *A bit less to scorn.*
>   *What have I done?*
>   *To what end was I born?*
>
> *To teach and delight.*
>   *Delight . . . or offend.*
>   *Luck's been no lady,*
>   *Truth a sneaky friend.*

Got the heater on full blast,
  Window jammed down,
  Odometer busted,
  Speedometer dead wrong:
Can't tell how fast I'm going,
Don't care how far I've gone.

from **THE HAZARDS OF IMAGERY**

The frescoes in the castle are by Pisano,
and they are so smooth and shining that
even today you can see your own reflection
in them.
                              —The Anonimo

IN THE HOUSE OF MESSER SCONFORTO

In the solarium can be found
a famous representation
of giants in chiaroscuro,
singing and dancing
and tromping about the earth.
It is called *Hymn to the Obvious.*
It is a mysterious work,
an audible darkness,
and it is unforgivable.

In the sanctuary, to the right
is an oil painting in which
Vitality is represented, wide-eyed
at the moment of waking, saluting
Death in the form of a toad
sitting on his belly.
It is an early example
of that type of brushwork
in which each stroke
is called a snarl.
Nevertheless, it, too,
is an unforgivable work,
scruffy and audacious,
cheerless and fireproof.

In the music room two busts
serve as a pair of bookends.
One portrays the young king
Mithridates
who, to make himself invulnerable
to assassins, sampled
poison every day; the other,
the old Mithridates,
who, when he desired to end
his life, could not find
a poison strong enough.
They are carved in stone.
Very hard stone.
But not that hard.

In the dining hall the group portrait
of a family weeping as they stand
over a puddle of milk
is by an unknown hand.
Many presume it is waterproof.
In fact, the application
of the slightest pressure reveals
it to be painted on an enormous sponge
that has recently been dunked.

In the mezzanine, Sprezzante
has painted *The Great Cramp*.
Is it Eternity, you ask, running
your fingertips across the cool wall,
or the loss of it?
Facing it is his masterpiece: *The Shrug*.

At The Palace Of The Seccatore

The oil paintings in the stable,
depictions of Trojans trying not
to look a gift horse in the mouth;
of Agamemnon biting off more
than he can chew; or Nimrod
beating around a bush;
of Hector biting the dust
on the plains of Troy;
the study of Nessus giving
the wife of Hercules
the shirt off his back;
the one of Nausicaa
refusing to touch Ulysses
with a ten-foot pole: these
are all soggy and stale,
but the risk of contagion
poses an empty threat.
I should also note that the frames
are surprisingly sturdy.

The landscape on the stairwell
is by Capopietro.
It portrays the fieldworkers
of Pietrosanto, stout,
broad-belted folk
who leave no stone unturned.

The lavish silk tapestry
in the studiolo was executed
over the course of ten years

by Pringle of Gint
and it depicts
The Twelve Sultry Steps
to a More Powerful Vocabulary.
The figures it includes
defy description.
So delicately woven are they
their faces appear imbrued
with a glum and sickly light,
the porcine squint of hedonists
corrupted, I suppose, by a life
lacking any impetus save comfort
and ease, where even the most
shallow pleasure proves enervating.
Their eyes look like withered pearls
interred in rheumy oysters.
These faces leave me disturbed
and confused, and at a loss for words.

At The Chapel Cardinal Finale

Here is a painting on wood
by an unknown hand,
of hearty fishermen in an open boat
hauling a cow out of the Bay of Naples.
This painting smells:
an unfortunate odor no one
can eradicate or name.

Here, too, is a painting of the Savior
from whose eyes many have attested
they have seen real tears fall.
And I for one believe it to be so.
For I have heard this said
of other paintings
and recalling how they are all
so unbelievably bad,
so poorly executed,
I have concluded that it is
the painters' utter ineptitude
that has made their very subjects weep.
Such is the miraculous power of art.

In The Gallery Of The Repeat Offenders

On the stairway's second landing
one must confront a painting
called *Feigned Injuries*.
Bearing many illegible signatures,
it portrays a full orchestra
over which ragged birds
fly in a blinding fog.
At one time there were those
who extracted ready meaning
from this award-winning work;
to do so now, one
must take a plunger to it.
Which for a few small coins
an attendant will provide.

In the main room there is
a magnificent carpet,
very valuable, very skillfully
embroidered, whose theme
is The One Hundred Most Frequently
Mispelled Words in the Language.
The weavers labored in poor light,
praying to St. Eugene,
patron saint of spelling
and penmanship, for guidance.
Despite evidence of spurning
along the edges, and a few
scowls and slurs and scoffs,
and perhaps a little searing

and scuffing here and there,
and sloshes and slashes
and dibs, it shows
no signs of retaliation.

Here, too, hangs a series
of suspiciously pristine pictures
whose titles I will now record:
The Ascension of the Drudge,
The Forgiveness of the Drudge,
The Redemption—, The Descent—,
and *The Agitation of the Drudge.*
After viewing these pictures
for a while, I do not know who I am.
I cease to wonder about things.
I go to the piazza
where I feed the pigeons,
humming half-familiar tunes
as the heavens grow dim.

At The Tomb Of The Improperly Trained Bombardiers

This is the saddest work I have ever seen.
A tremendous concrete piano,
its maker unknown, yet
—O soul of man! unutterable sorrow!
Impenetrable silence!
The Great Echo!

The poems framed in the corridor
are by Maginot.
They are thick, the lines
impenetrable, true *vers Maginot*,
and visitors are advised
to simply go around them.

AT THE PALACE OF MESSER MASSIMO

In the nursery the great canvas
that looms over the little cribs
and has as its subjects
The Modesty of Attila,
The Gumption of Achilles,
and famous conflagrations at sea,
is by Crassvoort of Holland.
The yellow smudge in the foreground
resembles a palm print,
but if viewed sideways
through a peephole in the frame,
it appears to be more than a smudge.
Not quite a swipe
but more like a smear.

The serene paintings opposite,
Infant Playing with Firearms
and *Mother Spreading Butter on a Melon*,
are, presumably, by that same artist.

The ceiling fresco looming
at an unfair height
over the dining room table,
a landscape that depicts mice
inspecting the skeleton
of an elk embedded in a frozen lake,
is thought by many to be the work
of Crassvoort the Younger.

The painting of Cupid, asleep
on his feet in the infernal regions,
is very old, but as
it includes a pregnant mule,
a flounder, chicken lips,
a squirrel with a crazed grin,
and other such accessories,
it is thought to have been restored
in the studio of Crassvoort.
The canvas is loosely framed,
in the Northern manner,
to resist pokes and jabs.
And so it has, for the most part.

At The Tavern Of Messer Angelo On La Via Canale

The colossal nudes, Hercules
and Voluptuousness on a seesaw;
the mezzo-relievo of youths
who have wreathed their heads
in roses to cool their brains
while drinking wine;
the figure of the Queen
of the Goths bouncing
the God of Apology off a tree:
these are all antique.

On a large canvas in the hallway
is an altogether remarkable work:
Venus reclines in the golden arms
of common day, her eyelids a bit weary,
her glowing thighs as slick as wet clay.

Various silk tapestries
hang free from the rafters,
the work of an artist
who kept his eyes not solely
on man working in the dust,
or on gods dreaming clouds on high,
but on the glowing rains
that hold them for an hour or so
in each other's thoughts.

One portrays Hermes, the glad god,
who moved faster than luck
or thought; who stole

what he could not himself create;
who first made music
—made it so effortlessly he seemed
to swipe it from the air—
and the first song he chose to sing
was a celebration of his own begetting.
(Trustworthy people have told me
that this work was filched
from The Tomb of the Secretary of Labor.)

Another, above the couch,
is said to represent
the devoted Lodovico, considering
the whorls of his lady's thumbprint
as a topographical map
of Mount Parnassus.

With the painting that shows Cupid
gazing into a mirror
that does not reflect his image,
Gaspari the Syrian poses
the question: When love can appear
so swiftly as to sneak up
on a mirror, how can mortals
and most gods defend themselves
against such a force?

AT THE COTTAGE OF MESSER VIOLI

The mailbox, painted dark blue,
sits atop a tilted cedar post.
It has a little red flag on one side
and it is altogether remarkable.

The Toyota in the driveway
is very old and is said
to have come from Japan.

There is in the hallway
an immense dog-food bowl.
It is made of iridescent pink plastic.
It is, as I have said, immense
and it is hideous.

In the kitchenette is a statuette
of Ceres, Goddess of Wheaties.

The dishwasher is a Kenmore
and altogether worthy of praise.

In the foyer the oversized painting
of a pork chop provides
visitors many opportunities
for conversation.

In the servants' quarters
there are many impressive works
that stress the imminence of death
and the probability of hellfire.

Placed on the broad maplewood table
beside bottles of cognac
there is a recording device
with a silver megaphone
into which natives may be
invited to shout
the oral histories of their people.

We, whose hearts have been gripped
by life, scoff at the idea of art
as mere ornamentation: So they
seem to proclaim,
the three statues that adorn
the neighbor's lawn, plaster deer
with real bullet holes in them.

Overnight

APPEAL TO THE GRAMMARIANS

We, the naturally hopeful,
Need a simple sign
For the myriad ways we're capsized.
We who love precise language
Need a finer way to convey
Disappointment and perplexity.
For speechlessness and all its inflections,
For upended expectations,
For every time we're ambushed
By trivial or stupefying irony,
For pure incredulity, we need
The inverted exclamation point.
For the dropped smile, the limp handshake,
For whoever has just unwrapped a dumb gift
Or taken the first sip of a flat beer,
Or felt love or pond ice
Give way underfoot, we deserve it.
We need it for the air pocket, the scratch shot,
The child whose ball doesn't bounce back,
The flat tire at journey's outset,
The odyssey that ends up in Weehawken.
But mainly because I need it—here and now
As I sit outside the Caffe Reggio
Staring at my espresso and cannoli
After this middle-aged couple
Came strolling by and he suddenly
Veered and sneezed all over my table
And she said to him, "See, *that's* why
I don't like to eat outside."

FINISH THESE SENTENCES

The qualities I look for in a subordinate are

A situation in which humor might be most unwelcome is

After considering which is better, to be wealthy or wise

My greatest sense of personal fulfillment depends on

It's one thing to champion a sticky empiricism
But it's another, altogether different thing to

I think of myself as a caring professional who as the days
And nights tumble by like woozy pandas trying to achieve
A position conducive to procreation

She had an accent that turned eyes to ice, heart
To hard, and transubstantiation to

From the bloody throats of those dull-colored birds
That scream at the sun,

As a patch of grass and wildflowers where lovers lay
Begins to revive, so too my mind once oppressed by joy

In that one moment when they begin to flap
Frantically in their doomed arc, the great books I fling
Off a high balcony almost

A complete individual is one who

Now there are hands, lovely hands that have played
Rare instruments in the dark and thrown
Many a burning basket into the wind, and there are eyes

I like to think my superiors value my ability to

It is easy for me first thing in the morning to scoff
At questions like how many angels can dance on a pinhead,
But such figments, especially when immersed in paradox,
Oxymora and the like, don't seem so frivolous when we
Recollect the most intense and memorable experiences of our
Lives, experiences that in one moment produce a state of
Devastating superflux, of many simultaneous, powerful and
Distinct if not contradictory feelings, that when captured
In words not only allow the closest thing to prayer that the
Faithless can rely on for solace, but also remind us how
Figurative speech provides a refined atavistic satisfaction,
Especially evident in the way deeply imagined metaphor by
Enlivening objects reawakens the residual susceptibility
Of the primitive, superstitious mind to fetishism and

AS I WAS TELLING DAVE AND ALEX KELLEY

My brother swears this is true.
And others have willingly—
Generously—testified,
As they did that other time when
After leaving an office party
They pulled off the expressway,
Walked into a place he'd never
Been to before, and ordered
A few more drinks while he
Headed for the lavatory.
But as he was crossing the dining room
On the other side of the bar
This vicious fight broke out.
Two women—well-dressed, tall,
Gorgeous—tore into each other,
Punching, clawing, swinging
Spike-heeled shoes, pulling
Each other's hair, and my brother,
Aghast, jumped between them
To break it up, grabbed them roughly,
Held them apart, berated
Them, tried to shake some sense
Into—when he gradually pieced
It all together: the changed look
On their faces, the disapproval,
The utter silence of condemnation
That everyone aimed not at the women
But at him, the fact that
It was a supper club theatre
And he had just jumped into
The climactic scene of a play—
But this, I hasten to add, is not

About my brother but his neighbor,
A man whose roof needed repair;
A man who, more than most, feared heights.
A ladder to this neighbor
Didn't ordinarily suggest the kind
Of elevating work that joins
The material to the spiritual,
So before mounting it he called
His children over and, as he wrapped
A rope thick enough to moor a barge
Around his waist and lashed
The other end around the car bumper,
Carefully explained to them
How they should steady the ladder
Until he had climbed onto the roof.
Up he went, not overstepping
But securing both feet on the same rung
Before proceeding to the next:
A trembling man on a trembling ladder.
He squirmed over the drain,
Crawled up the not very steep slope,
Flopped over the peak, then slid
Inch by inch down the rear slope
Until he felt confident enough
To kneel instead of crawl,
To sigh and take a deep breath
Before he began to cut a shingle.
Perhaps the first horripilating signal
Was a subtle tug on the rope,
Like an angel plucking a harp string.
Perhaps it was a sudden tautness
Around his waist, or, perhaps,

He heard the station wagon door
Slam shut, then the ignition,
The engine roar to life, or
Slowly, grindingly churn before it
Kicked in and he was yanked heavenward
Then jerked back, slammed, twisted,
Keelhauled belly up, belly down,
Over the roof, dashed onto the driveway
To be dragged, dribbled,
Bounced hard along the road, his
Wife looking this way and that
As she drove on, wondering
Wherever were those screams coming from?
Doctors, police, all believed
She could very well have not seen
The rope; could not, with windows
Rolled up, have ascertained,
While they lasted, the source,
Proximity and intensity of the screams.
And I, for one, though respectful
Of the family's desire for privacy,
Think for numerous, inevitable,
Irresistible, philosophical,
Sociological but mostly religious
Reasons, this place, this event,
This man deserves a shrine
Which, if donations are forthcoming,
I am willing to oversee
The construction of
At 145 Sampson Avenue,
Islip, Long Island, New York.
That's right, that's the name
Of the place: Islip. I swear.

I.D.

Or, Mistaken Identities

1.

To the island of my birth I returned
And spent my days
Taking life a thought at a time.
But no sooner would I squash
The life out of one thought
Than another jumped in.
Where did it get me,
A blind old man on the docks,
Staring beyond the sound of waves,
Pestering fishermen for stories,
Any story of the sea?
Hearing boys ship their oars,
Curse their snagged nets,
I asked them, "How did it go?
What did you catch?"
Only to have some wiseacre
Toss a riddle at me:
"We threw away what we caught.
What we didn't catch,
We kept them all."
That shut me up, stumped
By a couple of twerps.
For the life of me
I couldn't figure it out.
I mean trying to figure it out was
What did me in. I trudged off,
Scratching my bald head,
Looking like a scowling fool.

Distracted, I slipped on the slick bank
And down I went, busted up on the rocks.
I survived for a few more days,
Still wondering.

Who am I?

2.

For sixty-two years my mother
Carried me in her womb, so
It was not very strange
That I was born with white hair,
Nor that thereafter
I always endeavored
To conceal myself from the world.
I became a librarian.
Years of scholarship led me
To believe that people
Should be firmly ruled
By benevolent sages.
I advocated simplicity,
Compassion, spontaneity
And obscurity
As the greatest virtues
And concluded that the best way
To live was to do
Nothing but remain pure and still.
I sought transformation.
Dismayed by corruption and disorder,
I decided to wander off
Into the outlands.
At my departure, the gatekeeper
Importuned me to write down my thoughts,
Which I did, spontaneously,
Producing a short,
Extraordinarily obscure book
On the greatness of little things.
No one heard from me again;
Countless millions have pondered my book.

Who am I?

3.

For handing over Philologus
To the widow of the man
I'd commanded him to murder
(She then made him slice off bits
Of his own flesh, roast them
And then eat them)—For this,
Plutarch commended me
For at least one act
Of understanding and decency.

Who am I?

4.

My training as a magician was ordinary:
Rigorous and unpleasant.
I performed various ceremonies
Mostly of a religio-sexual nature
To promote fishing and cultivation.
I fostered vague beliefs in an array
Of powerful beings, most of whom
Were mischievous and stupid.
Transmigration into animals
Was my specialty.
It was a demanding job:
The spirits of my ancient ancestors
Control such practices but,
A cantankerous lot, they
Often withheld their favors.
I left my body after I died
And traveled to an unknown Western isle
Where to my relief
There were no deities,
Nor any conception of one, for that matter.
These days I return occasionally
To my former homeland
To marry a gorgeous mortal.
My nickname is "Frizzy."

Who am I?

5.

I always promised less
Than I knew I could deliver.
I made every favor
A surprise or a tribute.
I always greeted the mighty
With what they needed:
A look of wonder.
I studied the lives of the great caliphs:
He whose harem was guarded
By 8,000 eunuchs, half of them
White, half of them black;
He who poured a thousand pearls
Over the head of his first bride;
He who used infants' skulls for candle-snuffers;
He who founded a wondrous city
Centered on the garden
Of a Christian hermit named Dad.
Not for nothing was I made vizier—
Vizier to the Fatamite Caliph Aziz,
He who craved Baalbec cherries
More than the most virile believers
Stranded in a waste of sand
Yearn for unmentionable things.
For him I ordered a flock of 600 pigeons
To be dispatched from Baalbec to Cairo,
Each of which carried attached
To either leg a little silk bag
Containing a cherry.
Eventually, I was slain by infidels
Who buried my head in a pigskin sack.

Who am I?

6.

I set my heart on serving my Lord,
So that to Paradise I could ascend,
That holy place where, so I'd heard,
The fun, the games and laughter never end.

Without my honey, I couldn't go there.
Separated from her, I'd only be sad.
She with the lovely face, the golden hair,
Without her there's no joy to be had.

But I don't mean this to sound so willful,
As if I'd risked eternal damnation.
I didn't *have* to see her beautiful
Figure, or have her soft glance fall on me.
I just prayed for a little consolation:
To see her standing there in all her glory.

Who am I?

7.

Taddeo Bernardi of Lucca
Invited me to supper.
He was wealthy but ridiculous,
A show-off, a big galoot.
I no sooner arrived than,
As if inducting me into Paradise,
He showed me a great room
Where luxuriant tapestries
Hung above a floor made
Of colorful stones laid
In the most intricate pattern
Of vines, branches and leaves.
I gazed around, admiring everything,
And then spit in his face.
He was flabbergasted and deeply hurt.
In a not insensitive tone of voice
I hastened to explain:
"I didn't know where else to spit
That would have offended you less."

Who am I?

8.

To repair my health
And our fellowship,
To help me overcome
What he called
My "self-indulgences,"
My dearest friend invited me
To join him and his sister
On a journey, a tour
To remote parts of Scotland.
At the time, I dreaded sleep.
The nightmares that terrified me
Were more vivid than anything
I saw with open eyes.
Suffering from addiction,
In love with a woman
I could never possess,
Dejected, jealous
Of my friend's accomplishment
Whilst my own creative power waned,
Estranged from him
And everyone I loved
. . . Mayhap, I should not have agreed
To accompany them.
We sat back to back on benches
That ran the length
Of an open carriage,
A laughable equipage yanked
About by a swayback mare.
It rained and rained and I had
To listen helplessly

To his irrepressible sister,
Who, thinking to lift
All our spirits, recited
His verses for mile upon mile.
We parted ways.
With little money, no change
Of clothes, and poor shoes,
This wayward sample of mortality
Walked 263 miles in eight days.
One night during that time,
Somewhere—O somewhere!—
In the company of strangers,
Suffering from hunger,
Bloody feet, hysterical fits,
Uncontrollable weeping,
Stomach pains, dreams
Of shame and terror,
I resolved to marry
My philosophical investigations
To the daily thrills and fears
Of my own extinction, and thus
Engender and engild the great book of my life!

Who am I?

9.

Try this on for size:
I'm driving, o.k.? I'm tired.
Busted muffler's shaking my teeth loose.
I worked late. Too much coffee.
Way too much coffee, o.k.?
I finally get home, o.k.?
I nod hello to the wife.
I'm standing in front of the TV.
You know what I mean,
Standing there, flipping channels.
But then there's this close-up,
A moon-faced kid lying on a floor, o.k.?
Her whole face fills the screen.
I mean, she's right there, jabbing away
At an electronic keyboard
With her tongue.
Her head's bobbing along
Up and down, back and forth
And she's poking hard
At the wet keys under her chin.
The camera moves back and so do I.
Don't get me wrong,
I wasn't frightened.
Hell, I was in Korea *and* 'Nam,
So you know what I mean, o.k.?
She's lying on a blue rug,
She's wearing a blue jumpsuit,
The studio's red, white and blue,
But she's got no arms or legs
And she's going fierce and crazy

Playing the *Star Spangled Banner*.
The audience is standing around her.
They're looking down, jaws hanging,
Hands folded, really quiet.
They don't know what to think, o.k.?
They're glancing at the m.c.
Hoping he'll tip them off, o.k.?
Then there's a close-up of the m.c.
There he is, Morton Downey, Jr.
Tears are spilling from his eyes
And running down his facial warts, o.k.?
This is a delicate moment.
The crescendo's building
And so is the suspense.
This babe, at any moment, she might lean
Too far into that last
Screeching note and turn turtle.
You know what I mean: belly up!
I can't take it, it's not just the coffee, o.k.?
I want to flee out the back door
Of the Home of the Brave.
I got to change channels.
I get this, I get that,
I get static, I get fuzz,
I get vertical horizontals.
Then I get a black and white re-run.
Here's this guy running out a back door,
Down an alley, into a street.
He's amazed at the sight
Of normal-looking people, o.k.?

He's dressed in futurismo leotards,
They're dressed regular.
He's a waylaid earthling, o.k.?
He keeps grabbing them:
"Quick! You've got to tell me,
Where am I? What planet is this?"
That's it, the show's over!
Just like that.
So I turn to the wife and say,
Is that how it ends?
All she wants to do is get drunk
And watch *Lost Weekend* again.
But I really want to know,
Is that how it ends?

Who am I?

10.

I was fired today by a man with a terrible stutter.
His name was Garcia and—clean-cut,
Starched white shirt, bland tie,
The look of a conniving altar boy—
I couldn't help but like him.
The news surprised me.
I thought he intended
To offer congratulations
For a couple of fortunate
Events that had befallen me.
But since I didn't need the job
I quickly regained my equanimity.
He, as usual, was quite tense.
So to proceed smoothly,
Not to say sympathetically,
And to try to put him at ease
I began to help him pronounce
Those words that were proving
Particularly troublesome.
At first I attempted to coax him along
With charade-like gestures,
But the more I tried to help
The more help he needed,
And I was soon completing phrases
For him, then supplying entire sentences.
This reached an unforeseen result:
I realized that I had fired myself,
Not "for ca-ca-ca-cause,
Buh-buh-buh-but puh-puh-puh-pol—"
"Policy?"

"Yes, puh-puh-puh-puh-pol—"
"Policy!"
When we agreed that the meeting
Had probably come to an end,
We both rose a little hesitantly
From our chairs, leaned
Toward each other over his desk
And almost shook hands.
I left, feeling sorry that, for some reason,
I'd always made that fellow nervous.

Who am I?

11.

I seemed so likeable, so pleasant.
Everyone agreed.
In truth, I smelled like an old leper.
I was a vile, scrawny coward
Who with my armor off or on
Had to be propped up
So I wouldn't fall and drown
Face down in a puddle.

I can't explain my renown.
Indeed, more than once
I left the battlefield
Wondering who had won
And what was lost.

I was either a stingy and nasty
Or a wildly generous host.
Whenever I went broke
I'd sell more land
To have more fun
With my freeloading troubadour pals.

Though I often didn't know
Who or where I was, debtors
Had no trouble finding me
If they had a good ear
—and a thirst!

I could never decide
What to call
The kinds of poems I wrote,
Never knew

What I was saying.
They were more
Of a mystery to me
Than I was to myself.

Though Marcabru
Saluted me,
And the great Peire d'Alvernhe,
I suffered fools
Whose praise left me
Unable to see
Anything better
In a mirror
Than a raw oyster
On a sun-baked rock.

But when lovely words
Caught me in a rush
Of music glad and bold,
Like birds burst into flight,
Like a fountain blown—like
A tree I once saw
(I don't know what kind)
Whose leaves—as heavy as velvet,
As soft and light
As a delicate hand—
Whose dark leaves
With their bright undersides
Burst upward in a wayward gust,
All I could say was
I exceed myself.
I sent my little birds to play

In the fount of all my grief and mirth,
Noble ladies whose replies
Bludgeoned me with subtleties.

Without ever having seen her, I fell
In love with one, the Countess of Urgell.
The poems I sent her
Every summer day and winter
Night, somehow convinced her
Of my worth.

But now—look at this!
Whatever it is, fast or slow
I've managed to finish it
Without an ending or a worry.

I wrote it without knowing
Where it was going
Or whether it was written
For the many or the few
Or the one (who

Could turn a vague joke
Into a sweet little mystery.
The one who
Long after her husband
Died, long after she became a nun,
Said her one regret
Was that she never let
Me touch her bare leg
With the back of my hand).

Who am I?

Answer Key

1. Homer
2. Lao-tze
3. Mark Antony
4. The Duke of Malu
5. Abdul Ibn Kazaam
6. Giacomo da Lentino
7. Castruccio Castracani
8. Silas Tompkins Cumberbacke
9. Newton Minnow
10. Larsen E. Whipsnade
11. Raimbaut d'Orange

TO DANTE ALIGHIERI

from Cecco Angiolieri

Dante, if I'm a lout, you're a lummox.
I mooch a snack, you barge into a feast.
I act snooty, you play the gaudy snob.
I pluck a sonnet out of the gutter,
You dump a new canto in Faeryland.
I'm amazed you haven't caught on by now:
I stay skinny to make you look fatter.
But competition makes us both losers.
You sound more like a blowhard and you're so
Easy to beat the game's become a bore.
I fear you might perform the miracle
That would wring the fun out of all my sins.
So, let's call it a draw. If not, think twice:
As the mud deepens, who's the gadfly . . . who the ox?

COUNTERMAN

What'll it be?

Roast beef on rye, with tomato and mayo.

Whaddaya want on it?

A swipe of mayo.
Pepper but no salt.

You got it. Roast beef on rye.
You want lettuce on that?

No. Just tomato and mayo.

Tomato and mayo. You got it.
. . . Salt and pepper?

No salt, just a little pepper.

You got it. No salt.
You want tomato.

Yes. Tomato. No lettuce.

No lettuce. You got it.
. . . No salt, right?

Right. No salt.

You got it. Pickle?

No, no pickle. Just tomato and mayo.
And pepper.

Pepper.

Yes, a little pepper.

Right. A little pepper.
No pickle.

Right. No pickle.

You got it.
Next!

Roast beef on whole wheat, please,
With lettuce, mayonnaise and a center slice
Of beefsteak tomato.
The lettuce splayed, if you will,
In a Beaux Arts derivative of classical acanthus,
And the roast beef, thinly sliced, folded
In a multifoil arrangement
That eschews Bragdonian pretensions
Or any idea of divine geometric projection
For that matter, but simply provides
A setting for the tomato
To form a medallion with a dab
Of mayonnaise as a fleuron.
And—as eclectic as this may sound—
If the mayonnaise can also be applied
Along the crust in a Vitruvian scroll
And as a festoon below the medallion,
That would be swell.

You mean like in the Cathedral St. Pierre in Geneva?

Yes, but the swag more like the one below the rosette
At the Royal Palace in Amsterdam.

You got it.
Next!

HOUSE OF XERXES

Here come those splendid Persians!
We were expecting fireworks
And here they are!
Short bows, long arrows, iron breastplates—
Nice fish-scale pattern on those breastplates.
Just the right beach touch, very decky.
Quivers dangling under wicker-worky shields,
A casual touch, that.
And those floppy felt caps
Make it all very wearable, very sporty.
Huge amounts of gold,
A killer-look feel
But it still says A Day at the Shore.

Now those bumping, thumping Assyrians.
A nice mix here: bronze helmets
Or plaited headgear.
Shields, spears, daggers, /
The iron studs on those wooden clubs
A subtle retro bit.
And right on their heels the Bactrians!
A sort of butch-and-bitch combo,
Not tidy, not prim, almost
A dare-to-wear outfit.
And look at that headgear!
Whatever were they thinking?
And the bows, cane bows
Bringing back that beach scene scream.
Somebody's been smitten by cane.

Tromping right along: Scythians with a scowl!
Plenty of flounce and pout but somehow
It all spells powerhouse.

Stiff, pointed helmets and loose trousers,
Bows, daggers, battle-axes:
Just look at these ratty party boys.
Itchy and raw, apocalyptic but functional.
Takes us away from the beach look
But how can you not love them?

Look at these Sarangae!
Are we ready for this?
A lot of lavender, a lot of white and blue,
Colorama glamorama.
A little raggedy, a little trashy
Yet a narrow silhouette.
Narrow but masculine for sure.
Just what are these boys up to?

Oh, now how can you not love
These madcap Ethiopians?
Leopard skins and lion pelts,
Spearheads made of gazelle horns.
Now that is a new twist.
And who thought of this—body paint!
Half white chalk, half ochre.
The all-around mix and match
A big directional, indeed.

Check out the headgear!
A horse's scalp
Including ears and mane
For cryin' out loud.
Very jaunty, very focused.
Somebody pinch me!

Now, good grief, are we ready for the Libyans?
The brocade scaled back, thank god.
A big sulky leather look.
It's a bomber-jacket feeling.
I get a bomber-jacket feeling from this.
Javelins with burnt tips, daggers,
Minimal action gear but spiffy.

Marching, tromping right in,
What a welcome
For the Paphlagonian cuties!
Shields, spears, javelins and daggers—
Overloaded you might say, but
Why in heaven's name not?

Get a load of what's been done
With the traditional booties:
Halfway up the shin.
A booty and greave combo.
Now how cute is that?
And everyone agrees
Under those plaited helmets
Those Paphlagonians
Have the curliest hair in the world.

Here come the Thracians.
Fox-skin caps, fawn-skin boots, wooden helmets,
You just know how great
Their gorgeous garb makes them feel.

And right on their heels—the Pisidae!
Another wardrobe pick-me-up.

Bronze helmets shaped
Into the ears and horns of an ox.
What a way to say: Surprise!
A very jaunty crest,
Red cloth leggings,
Fashionable yet functional,
Smart but approachable,
Sporty in a tongue-in-chic sort of way.

You don't want to miss this!
Barefoot Sagartians, with lariats!
No optionals, nothing but lariats.
Now that is new.
No fashion fears here.
The total look flouncy, loose and extra large.

Turbaned Cyprians
With high high high high greaves!
Dangling daggers, billhooks!
Untreated ox-hide vests.
Something we'd want in our closet.
Lion, tiger, fox and ox: the full idiom.
Upbeat and very wearable,
A dose of novelty, a dose
Of frivolity—a definite smash.

They are having a good time up there.
Rough and raw yet a lot of flash.
Lavish, zippy, sleek.
Where is it all going?
An etude for today's world.
A dressy apocalyptic beach look.

A high-octane action look.
A premium blend of guts
And sass and imagination.
Feel the frenzy.
A big round of applause for the whole spectrum,
For a very big directional
That can't help but whip it up.
Who's able to take it all in?
Everyone's breathless.
Today we're making history.
We're raising Cain.

TOWARD A FEBRUARY SONGBOOK

A whirl of icy snow
Over fallen leaves could be a scrape
Or a caress, whisper or hiss.
A burning hiss or a buzz.
Dense oak, a few pine, a few rampike.
A nearly heart-shaped stone.
The one great beech, an eons-old nudge
From its sharkskin bark.
Low walls, neatly stacked then thrown
Into a sloppy heap the higher uphill they go.
Deadfall strewn willy-nilly
Like an abandoned game of pick-up sticks.
The thickly wooded land,
The very thought of the brutal work
It once took to clear it—soon enough
The entire hillside will be buried
In greenery, the low stream will leap
Back into itself and guzzle away, but now,
Ah, now February is springtime for gray
And I'm at my lighthearted best.
Heart as light as a hornet's nest.

WRITTEN IN A TIME OF WORRY AND WOE

I stopped and leaned over the footbridge rail.
Far below, roaring by the library,
The stream plunged through deep winter with the force
That follows a spring thaw, re-enacting
In a short stretch its ever-varied course.
I watched it flow clear under clear black ice,
Churn frothy under gray, tunnel and swirl
Under snow, pool and spill, then slide over
And under overturned stumps and debris.
I watched until I thought: February—
The apex of the year, and felt so far
Above the sum of whatever I've known
Or seen or done that I couldn't care less
What I must have lost to feel so cold and free.

ACKNOWLEDGMENTS

A month of twilights, laglight, fritterdusk. Withered plants, soggy bulbs, stubble. The Garden in February. Mold and tendrils, colorless scribbles dangling from a ripped-back carpet of matted leaves. Fresh hole in the frozen ground that looks like it was made by a pickaxe, a fang. Smeared dirt and frost, diamond slime. Paradise a child's notion. Paradise painted one stroke, one phrase, one glimpse at a time, whatever a lightning flare reveals of it. Blunderblink. An invitation. Mr. and Mrs. Dwindle. Request. Demand. The pleasure of your company, your antics, your fervor, your moodiness, your stolid numbing small-time solemnity, your contempt, your pigheaded pride, your carelessness, your squalling self.

PANORAMA

"My films never end, they never have
a simple solution."

Fellini, you must be alive at this hour.
Behind the scenes, calling the shots.
While I'm waiting behind the wheel,
Trying to decide whether to let the car
Warm up more or get going before
The roads get worse, this winged zero
Soars out of the night snow
And (Extreme Close-up) slams me in the face.
Nice touch, Maestro!
Ten minutes ago I was sailing
Through class, throwing out what I know
As if bailing out a boat.
Now what am I supposed to do?
Stare out at this dull town
Now that for no reason, not even
Mere weariness, any faith or delight
Has been blown away like ashes
In the wild and brilliant snow
That has left Bloomfield vacant
(Extreme Long Shot), closed it down
But for one pizza shop, a fluorescent blank
(Medium Shot) across the avenue, so
Picture-perfect it seems fake,
Except for the waitresses and waiters
(Medium Close-up) in their black skirts
And pants and white blouses and T-shirts
Who stare like mourners into the night
Until one has sense enough to toss

A piece of crust at the one
Wiping the lid (Extreme Close-up)
Of the giant oven and another flicks
A spoonful of flour at a waitress
Who scoops up a pile with both hands
And (Wide Shot) splashes him down
(Close-up) before he twirls a floppy lasso
Of dough across the marble counter
And the air (Wide Shot) blooms
With doughballs and napkins, dishrags
And flour (Medium Close-up) and out
The door they fly in whiteface
And run and jump, dance and tumble
In each other's arms and the whirling
Air (Wide Shot) as I roll slowly
By them (Tracking Out), simple as that.

THIEF TEMPTED BY THE GRANDEUR OF FEBRUARY

Wake up! I can't wait to tell you
How much I learned in my sleep.
And though I remain somewhat modest
And completely charming,
I have indeed changed.

Do you know that taxidermy students
Begin with a mastodon
And end by stuffing a flea?
And as for poetry, it's easy
And impossible—like stealing from yourself.

Do you know that whenever a weatherman
Grows alarmingly unpredictable,
As long as he retains
A bit of modesty and charm,
He's promoted to astronomer?

And that like an astronomer in the mist,
I am coaxed onward, in love
With the blessings of sleep,
The lustre of sleeplessness, more and more
Aware of how serious I've become
Because of you—serious
And yet somehow remarkably pleasant.

The beauties of the night, I already know
What it's like to feel cold
And beautiful hair slide through my hands.
Beyond the edge of forgetfulness
Or the last of a fine rain,
A few memories flare

And sputter in a final appeal.
What once seemed true,
What once seemed wrong,
I let them disappear, blown away
By a caress, a spray of light here
And there across slick, wide avenues.
Distant pleasures, distant strife,
I now can say, modestly
But not without significant charm,
I know the errors of my life.

Paul Violi: A Brief Chronology

1944	Paul Randolph Violi born in New York on July 20.
to 1962	Violi grows up in Greenlawn, on the North Shore of Long Island.
1962-66	Attends Boston University; graduates with a B.A. in English and a minor in Art History.
Dec. 1966- June 1967	Joins Peace Corps; sent to northern Nigeria to work as surveyor and mapmaker. Leaves at the onset of Biafran revolt.
June 1967- Apr. 1968	From Nigeria, with minimal funds, travels to Ivory Coast, Senegal, the Canary Islands, Spain, Italy, Greece, Bulgaria, Turkey, Iran, Afghanistan, Pakistan, India, and Nepal, and then back to Europe. Flies from Amsterdam to New York on April 9; settles in Manhattan's East Village.
1968	Holds a number of short-lived jobs: clam-digging in Long Island's Great South Bay; on the cruise ship *Franconia*; as a sales representative for Thomas Cook Tours; and at CBS-TV News at the dispatch desk (into 1969).
1969	In April, through a mutual friend, gets in touch with Ann Boylston (whom he had briefly dated in high school); they become romantically involved and marry on June 29. Beginning in the summer—and over the next three years—attends workshops at the Poetry Project at St. Mark's Church, including those conducted by Dick Gallup, Carter Ratcliff, Peter Schjeldahl, and Tony Towle. Takes a job as a political pollster.
1970	In the spring semester of Towle's workshop, meets Charles North, and also Alan Appel, with whom he edits four issues of a little magazine, *New York Times*, under the imprint of The Swollen Magpie Press. In the fall, moves with Ann to Beacon, New York. Self-publishes two chapbooks through Swollen Magpie: *She'll Be Riding Six White Horses*

and *Automatic Transmissions*. By 1982, these two publications would be dropped from his list of previously published titles. Joins the editorial staff of a new weekly newspaper, *The Herald*, where he works until 1972.

1972   Daughter, Helen, born January 2. Moves family from Beacon to Briarcliff. Works at *Architectural Forum* as Managing Editor (until 1974). Allen Kornblum's Toothpaste Press publishes *Waterworks*.

1973   Lita Hornick's Kulchur Foundation publishes his first substantial collection, the 120-page *In Baltic Circles*.

1974   Conducts poetry workshop at the Poetry Project at St. Mark's for the 1974-75 season. As chairman of the Museum of Modern Art's Associate Council Poetry Committee, helps organize poetry readings at MoMA over the next nine years. Works at *Merchandising Week* as "major appliance" editor.

1975   Takes first teaching position (part-time), at Bloomfield College, Bloomfield, New Jersey. Over the next twenty-five years, in addition to Bloomfield, he teaches at New York University, Scarsdale Teachers Institute, SUNY Purchase, the Dalton School, and Pace University White Plains, as well as in public schools, and conducts numerous poetry workshops in high schools under the auspices of Poets & Writers. Works on special projects at Universal Limited Art Editions, including helping Buckminster Fuller organize the text for his lithographic book, *Tetrascroll*. Works as associate editor at *Chainstore Age* magazine.

1976   Publishes *Some Poems* through Swollen Magpie Press (only *Poems* appears on the cover), which he prints at Bob Hershon's nonprofit The Print Center, in Brooklyn. (Hershon is also an editor of Hanging Loose Press, which will publish Violi in the future.) Works as test proctor for College of Financial Planning (annually until 1984).

1977   Finishes *Harmatan*, a book-length poem about his experiences in
        Nigeria (early sketches of which had appeared in *She'll Be Riding Six
        White Horses* and *In Baltic Circles*), which Bill Zavatsky publishes
        through his press, SUN. Moves with family to Putnam Valley, New
        York; son, Alexander, born August 30. Expands Swollen Magpie, with
        Charles North as co-editor/publisher, producing ten books between
        1977 and 1982, including poetry by Tony Towle, Joseph Ceravolo,
        Mary Ferrari, and Yuki Hartman, and the poet/painter anthology
        Broadway (co-edited by North and James Schuyler). Serves as Interim
        Director of The Poetry Project.

1978   Receives New York Creative Artists Public Service Fund (CAPS)
        Poetry Fellowship.

1979   Receives an Ingram Merrill Foundation grant.

1980   Receives a National Endowment for the Arts Poetry Fellowship.

1980s   Works as freelance copyeditor for The Franklin Mint.

1982   SUN publishes *Splurge*.

1986   Receives a National Endowment for the Arts Poetry Fellowship.

1987   Receives a New York Foundation for the Arts Poetry Fellowship.

1988   Hanging Loose Press publishes *Likewise*. Receives a Fund for Poetry grant.

1992   Receives a Fund for Poetry grant.

1993   Curates (and writes a catalog essay for) *Kenneth Koch: Collaborations
        with Artists*, exhibited at Christchurch Mansion, Ipswich, U.K. Both Violi
        and Koch attend the opening, and afterward give a series of poetry

readings together in England, as well as travel to the Lake District. Hanging Loose publishes *The Curious Builder*. In the summer, is hired to operate Harvester machine to remove invasive weeds from local lake (also in 1994).

1995 Yanni Florence and Leo Edelstein's Pataphysics Press (Melbourne, Australia) publishes *The Anamorphosis* (later included in *Fracas*), with drawings by Dale Devereux Barker.

1999 Hanging Loose publishes *Fracas*.

2000 Begins teaching at Columbia University. Coffee House Press publishes *Breakers*, a selection of longer poems.

2001 Receives Morton Dauwen Zabel Award from the Academy of Arts and Letters. Receives a Foundation for Contemporary Arts Poetry Award.

2002 Hanging Loose publishes a book of prose stories and sketches, *Selected Accidents, Pointless Anecdotes*.

2003 Begins teaching in the MFA poetry program at New School University, and over the next eight years develops an enthusiastic and loyal following of students.

2004 Receives John Ciardi Lifetime Achievement Award in Poetry from *Italian Americana* and the National Italian American Foundation.

2005 The Black Shed Press (Ipswich, U.K.) publishes *Envoy: Life Is Completely Interesting* (later appearing in *Overnight* as "Envoy"), with drawings by Dale Devereux Barker.

2007   Hanging Loose publishes *Overnight*.

2011   Diagnosed with pancreatic cancer in January. Dies at Hudson Valley
            Hospital, Cortland Manor, New York, on April 2. *In Baltic Circles*
            reprinted by Nate Pritts and Matt Hart's H_NGM_N BKS.

2014   Hanging Loose publishes *The Tame Magpie*, a selection of poems
            written since *Overnight*.